Personnel Administration in the Christian School

Personnel Administration in the Christian School

To Marlin
Matt. 20:25-28
Brubaker

J. Lester Brubaker

J. Lester

BMH Books
Winona Lake, Indiana 46590

Cover design by Jane Fretz

First printing, May 1980
Second printing, February 1981
Third printing, July 1983

ISBN: 0-88469-130-6

Printed in U.S.A.

To

the students in my class
in Personnel Management at
Grace Theological Seminary
June 1975
who planted in my mind
the seed-idea for this book.

Foreword

There is nothing more critical to the effective operation of any institution than to have competent and enthusiastic people working harmoniously together. The wise administrator realizes that his most important task is the identification, recruitment, and development of a committed Christian faculty and staff. That is what this book is all about.

The growth of the Christian school movement in recent years has been phenomenal. We rejoice in the increased opportunities for boys and girls all over the nation to attend Christian schools. At the same time, we are concerned about the total impact of the experiences that will be theirs in those schools. Schools, like the teachers who serve them, have personalities. They create an atmosphere and communicate to the students and others the character of Christian life and work. The kind of teachers and staff they encounter will determine the extent to which the impact of schooling will be positive and productive in the lives of the young people who attend.

It was out of such concern for the effective operation and testimony of Christian schools that this book was born. Dr. Brubaker so effectively communicated this concern to his students in our graduate program in Christian School Administration that they urged him to publish the material so others could benefit from his counsel. In writing this book, Dr. Brubaker has drawn upon many years of experience as a Christian educator and administrator. In this book—as in his summer classes at Grace Theological Seminary—Dr. Brubaker has beautifully combined the theoretical and the practical in the application of relevent biblical principles.

This book is not for everyone, but it should be required reading for every administrator and prospective administrator of a Christian school. Wise administrators will keep a copy handy for reference purposes. School board members would also benefit from reading it.

The beneficiaries of this book will not only be the administrators, but also the teachers and those who staff our Christian schools. Then, too, the children for whom the schools are established will be helped by the quality of instruction and the consistent, unified testimony that results from a knowledgeable and dedicated administration. Parents and friends of Christian schools will also support them more enthusiastically. The final result will be that our Lord, whose name we and our schools proudly bear, will be glorified.

Dr. E. William Male
Dean, Grace Theological Seminary

Preface

In 1975 I taught Personnel Management in the second summer of the M.A. program in Christian School Administration at Grace College and Seminary, Winona Lake, Indiana. At the close of the course several students came to me, urging that I put my lectures into textbook form. Out of this urging and with time provided by a sabbatical leave from Lancaster Mennonite High School, I have gathered information that I believe will be useful to administrators of Christian schools.

This is not a textbook on school administration. Neither is it a manual on leadership. It is an "in-between" book, providing suggestions for administrative policies and procedures that will free employees to do their best and to be happy in the work to which the Lord has called them. Relationships are emphasized, for they are the heart of personnel administration.

On the facing page of each chapter beginning, several Scripture verses are quoted for their devotional relevance to the topic that follows.

Because the English language has not yet developed a satisfactory single pronoun denoting male or female, the traditional forms have been used. They are not meant to imply masculine gender.

Unless otherwise noted, all Scripture quotations are from the New International Version.

I am grateful to my wife, Lois, for her encouragement in this project; to my colleagues at Lancaster Mennonite High School for teaching me many things; to J. Richard Thomas, assistant principal, and Larry W. Newswanger, former board member, for critical review of the manuscript; to Dr. Roy W. Lowrie, Jr., president of the Association of Christian Schools International and headmaster of Delaware County Christian School, for suggestions; and to Dr. E. William Male, dean of Grace Theological Seminary, for writing the foreword.

–J. Lester Brubaker
Superintendent, Lancaster Mennonite High School
2176 Lincoln Highway East
Lancaster, PA 17602

Table of Contents

~~~~~~

Introduction

"In those days Israel had no king; everyone did as he saw fit" (Judges 17:6).

"I, wisdom, dwell together with prudence; I possess knowledge and discretion.... Counsel and sound judgment are mine; I have understanding and power" (Prov. 8:12, 14).

"So he said to me, 'This is the word of the LORD to Zerubbabel: "Not by might nor by power, but by my Spirit," says the LORD almighty' " (Zech. 4:6).

"Very early in the morning, while it was still dark, Jesus got up, left the house and went off to a solitary place, where he prayed" (Mark 1:35).

"If any of you lacks wisdom, he should ask God, who gives generously to all without finding fault, and it will be given to him. But when he asks, he must believe and not doubt, because he who doubts is like a wave of the sea, blown and tossed by the wind. That man should not think he will receive anything from the Lord; he is a double-minded man, unstable in all he does" (James 1:5-8).

"But the wisdom that comes from heaven is first of all pure; then peace loving, considerate, submissive, full of mercy and good fruit, impartial and sincere. Peacemakers who sow in peace raise a harvest of righteousness" (James 3:17-18).

1. Overview of the Personnel Administration Function

"The body is a unit, though it is made up of many parts; and though all its parts are many, they form one body.... "Now the body is not made up of one part but of many. If the foot should say, 'Because I am not a hand, I do not belong to the body,' it would not for that reason cease to be part of the body. And if the ear should say, 'Because I am not an eye, I do not belong to the body,' it would not for that reason cease to be part of the body. If the whole body were an eye, where would the sense of hearing be? If the whole body were an ear, where would the sense of smell be? But in fact God has arranged the parts in the body, every one of them, just as he wanted them to be. If they were all one part, where would the body be? As it is, there are many parts, but one body.

"The eye cannot say to the hand, 'I don't need you!' And the head cannot say to the feet, 'I don't need you!' On the contrary, those parts of the body that seem to be weaker are indispensable, and the parts that we think are less honorable we treat with special honor. And the parts that are unpresentable are treated with special modesty, while our presentable parts need no special treatment. But God has combined the members of the body and has given greater honor to the parts that lacked it, so that there should be no division in the body, but that its parts should have equal concern for each other. If one part suffers, every part suffers with it; if one part is honored, every part rejoices with it" (1 Cor. 12:12, 14-26).

"But God has harmonized the whole body by giving importance of function to the parts which lack apparent importance, that the body should work together as a whole with all the members in sympathetic relationship with one another" (1 Cor. 12:24-25 Phillips).

The Analogy of the Body

In the Christian school, as in the church, there are a variety of tasks to be performed. For efficiency of operation these tasks are best assigned to those most gifted to perform each one. The person who oversees the assignment and performance of tasks is called the administrator; the function he performs in enabling each to work effectively and harmoniously within "the body" or staff is personnel administration.

Instructional Goals and Human Relations

Personnel administration is concerned with achieving the goals of the institution. Goals are met through people and the quality of their relationships. The personnel administrator needs to focus his attention on goals and personnel simultaneously.

Lee M. Yoder, vice president for administrative affairs at Eastern Mennonite College, describes personnel administration in this way:

> Personnel management to me means helping people understand their job descriptions, their responsibilities, and their reporting procedures so that together we can eliminate the ambiguities, the uncertainties connected to our work—so that we can be open with each other.[1]

Definition and Functions of Personnel Administration

Personnel administration is that aspect of the total administrative task that has to do with determining personnel needs, filling personnel needs, and servicing personnel employed so that all employees can happily and effectively help the school to achieve its goals.

William B. Castetter describes the function of personnel administration as facilitating "achievement of system goals through human agents."[2] Jay E. Greene provides the following description:

> The functions of the school personnel administrator may be grouped under four headings. First is the process of staffing the schools. It may include recruitment, selection, assignment, promotion, service termination and retirement. The second function is the process of developing a personnel policy. Normally, it involves working with employee groups within policies set by the board of education and the school superintendent to develop those conditions of employment in which an optimum teaching environment and attitude can be developed. The third function is that of stimulating and developing staff morale. It involves skill in human relations, giving recognition for service performed with high quality, and releasing the creative capacity of all staff members. Fourth is the process of providing services for staff. It is closely related to staff morale and involves personal counseling, insurance and retirement considerations, and in-service education.[3]

Greene also suggests that the personnel function can be viewed from the perspective of allocations: "The allocation of persons to positions and the allocation of rewards in return for their services. The allocating process may be viewed in three stages which are analytically rather clear, namely, entrance into the system (hiring), service to the system (employment), and departure from the system (withdrawal)."[4]

Normally in the Christian school the personnel function will be carried out by the chief school officer. He may carry a title such as principal, superintendent, or headmaster. In many cases he will be the only administrator in the school. Only when a school is operated as a system in several buildings with thousands of pupils is there need for a special personnel administrator. For the sake of simplicity and consistency, the term "principal" will be used hereafter to designate the chief school administrator.

The Principal as Leader

Because the principal of the Christian school carries the major administrative load (and sometimes the entire load), it is especially important that he be chosen carefully by the board. For him to be an effective personnel administrator he must have leadership qualities that enable him to work harmoniously with other people. The Bible mentions traits that qualify one to be a leader. The following list are examples from the New Testament only:

Prayerfulness—"One of those days Jesus went out into the hills to pray, and spent the night praying to God" (Luke 6:12).

Ability to delegate—"After this the Lord appointed seventy-two others and sent them two by two ahead of him to every town and place where he was about to go" (Luke 10:1).

Human insight—"But Jesus would not entrust himself to them, for he knew all men. He did not need man's testimony about man, for he knew what was in a man" (John 2:24-25).

Humility—"He must become greater; I must become less important" (John 3:30).

Love—"Having loved his own who were in the world, he [Jesus] now showed them the full extent of his love" (John 13:1).

Courage—"When they saw the courage of Peter and John and realized that they were unschooled, ordinary men, they were astonished and they took note that these men had been with Jesus" (Acts 4:13).

Spirit-infilling—"Brothers, choose seven men from among you who are known to be full of the Spirit and wisdom" (Acts 6:3).

Wisdom—(Acts 6:3 above).

Sympathy—"We who are strong ought to bear with the failings of the weak, and not to please ourselves" (Rom. 15:1).

Self-discipline—"Now the overseer must be above reproach, the husband of but one wife, temperate, self-controlled, respectable, hospitable, able to teach" (1 Tim. 3:2).

Good reputation—"He must also have a good reputation with outsiders, so that he will not fall into disgrace and into the devil's trap" (1 Tim. 3:7).

Gentleness—"And the Lord's servant must not quarrel; instead, he must be kind [gentle KJV] to everyone, able to teach, not resentful" (2 Tim. 2:24).

Ability to teach—(1 Tim. 3:2 above).

Faith—(Heb. 11).

Role of the School Board in Personnel Administration

The role of the school board in personnel administration is to establish the policies that will enable the principal to build and maintain a quality staff. Boards need to avoid the temptation to administer either personnel or program. They hire a competent principal to do these things for them. Nevertheless, he needs the guidelines of board policies so that he can act for them in the best interests of the school and its employees.

Building the
School Staff

"When Jesus saw the crowd around him, he gave orders to cross to the other side of the lake. Then a teacher of the law came to him and said, 'Teacher, I will follow you wherever you go.'

"Jesus replied, 'Foxes have holes and birds of the air have nests, but the Son of Man has no place to lay his head.'

"Another man, one of his disciples, said to him, 'Lord, first let me go and bury my father.'

"But Jesus told him, 'Follow me, and let the dead bury their own dead.'

"Then he got into the boat and his disciples followed him" (Matt. 8:18-23).

"When he saw the crowds, he had compassion on them, because they were harassed and helpless, like sheep without a shepherd. Then he said to his disciples, 'The harvest is plentiful but the workers are few' " (Matt. 9:36-37).

"As he walked along, he saw Levi son of Alphaeus sitting at the tax collector's booth. 'Follow me,' Jesus told him, and Levi got up and followed him" (Mark 2:14).

"So the Twelve gathered all the disciples together and said, 'It would not be right for us to neglect the ministry of the word of God in order to wait on tables. Brothers, choose seven men from among you who are known to be full of the Spirit and wisdom. We will turn this responsibility over to them and will give our attention to prayer and the ministry of the word' " (Acts 6:2-4).

2. Recruitment

Recruitment is the first step in obtaining a quality staff for the Christian school. The wise principal has a planned program of staff recruitment that he actively pursues. He has developed the program through study, observation, counsel, and prayer. He enters into recruitment activities with a deep sense of dependence upon God for guidance and discerning wisdom.

Supply and Demand

In the 1970s public schools were experiencing an oversupply of prospective teachers for the positions available. Only a few specialized fields were in short supply. Factors causing this oversupply were many and complexly interrelated; some were temporary. Among the factors were (1) economic squeeze on schools caused by inflation, reduction in federal aid, and taxpayer revolt against increasing taxes; (2) fewer pupils caused by a declining birth rate; and (3) fewer teachers leaving the profession, caused by a need to maintain job security.

These factors have not affected Christian schools in the same way. New schools have been opening. Established schools have burgeoning enrollments. Competent teachers with the spiritual qualifications and commitments required by boards of Christian schools remain in short supply.

At times the quality of candidates for positions in Christian schools leaves something to be desired. There are those whose personal commitment to Christ gives them a strong motivation to follow a "service" vocation; teaching seems most suitable for a variety of reasons. It is difficult to convince some of these people that emotional stability, academic competence, positive interpersonal relationships, and teaching skill are also requirements. Perhaps more difficult is the task of helping a particular candidate recognize such personal inadequacies in himself, without his being emotionally crushed. Teacher educators and school principals must stand firm in the awareness that dedication to Christ is no substitute for competence, but they must take this stand compassionately.

Board Policies

To give both guidance and freedom for the administration of recruitment efforts the school board needs to establish policies in this area. Such policy questions as these require answers:

Who does the work of recruitment?

Where and how shall it be done?

Who pays the expenses?

How much freedom does the recruiter have in making decisions?

What qualifications are required in candidates?

Who does it? In some Christian schools board members do the recruiting of teachers. They interview on college campuses and make other contacts with possible employees. Some do this in company with their principal; others do not involve the principal at all.

School boards should establish policies that clearly designate the principal as their recruitment agent. The principal should, however, be receptive to suggestions from the board. If the board lacks confidence in the principal's ability to function as their recruitment agent, they need to replace him with a person they will trust. Recruitment is a function of administration; establishing the framework for operation is a board function.

Where and how? To answer this question the board needs to determine the kind of persons being sought. Are certain doctrinal positions required? Is membership in a particular denomination a requisite? Is prior teaching experience necessary? The answers to such questions help determine whether recruitment shall be done on certain college campuses, at certain Bible institutes or colleges, or by seeking out experienced candidates only. Some boards may be comfortable establishing a priority listing of sources for faculty.

Who pays? Recruitment can be costly if it involves a great deal of travel to Christian teacher-preparing institutions or visits of candidates to the employing school. How much may the principal spend for his own travel? Do candidates receive full, partial, or no remuneration for visits to the school? A board needs policies that answer such questions. In addition, it is helpful for the annual budget to include an appropriation for recruitment expenses.

How much freedom? Principals sometimes feel handicapped in recruiting because they can give little clarifying information on recruitment visits without checking back with their boards. Candidates lose interest because the interviewer is vague in response to their questions.

Recruitment Factors—Long-Range

Staff morale. The way staff members feel about the school and interpersonal relationships on the staff affect recruitment in various ways. It is difficult for a principal to be enthusiastic if he knows faculty morale is sagging or that there is backbiting and other unchristian behavior among staff persons. A candidate who visits the school often senses rather quickly when teachers have negative feelings and low morale. A professional man in another field commented after visiting a Christian school: "How can they teach any positive values there? All that I heard among the faculty was complaining about low salaries."

Reputation of the school. The impression outsiders have of a school may be highly inaccurate but it affects staff recruitment. For example, an alumnus of a particular Christian school is enrolled in a college which is being visited by that Christian school's recruiter. The number of college students to sign up for interviews with the visiting recruiter is influenced by the image of the school given to the candidate through association with the alumnus of the school. The quality of the alumnus's Christian living and his attitudes toward his former school prejudice the candidate favorably or unfavorably regarding the desirability of teaching in the school. Again, someone visits a Christian school, is impressed, and spreads the word to his friends: "That's a good school."

Staff morale and school reputation generally yield to change slowly. An effective principal is aware of elements that affect reputation and morale and has a program of improvement.

Long-range personnel planning. An alert principal plans not only for the next year but for several years ahead. He will know when the growing school will be adding grade five, or a guidance office, or a program for the learning disabled. He will publicize personnel needs in advance. He will keep a file of names of persons whom he would like to attract to his staff. One principal tells such persons: "If you ever sense the cloud of the Lord's direction moving you away from where you are, contact me." At Lancaster Mennonite High School several persons have been employed who could not come at the first invitation. The principal kept in touch for a year or several years and so added outstanding experienced teachers to the staff.

Recruitment Factors—Short-Range

College visits. A principal ought to pay an annual recruitment visit to Christian liberal arts colleges and Bible colleges that graduate the kind of candidates he and the board desire. Placement offices of these institutions are generally eager to provide service in setting up appropriate interview facilities if they are contacted several weeks in advance. Be specific in telling them the grade level and/or subject fields for which you are recruiting.

Many times a close contact between the principal and the college will bring invitations to speak in chapel, to education classes, or to conduct seminars on Christian schools. Such exposure has both immediate and long-term benefits in personnel recruitment.

Promotional materials. A good general-purpose brochure that describes the school positively but honestly is helpful in recruitment. Candidates find copies of the student handbook useful in helping them understand the school philosophy and the patterns of living that are important at the school. Special recruitment "viewbooks" are an unjustified expense for small Christian schools. They might also suggest a "Madison Avenue super-sell" approach that is incompatible with Christian ideals.

Advertising and announcements. The value of advertising staff needs will vary with school situations. It can be helpful if one has access to a periodical that serves a large part of the supporting constituency. An ad placed in a denominational magazine or in an evangelical publication may be inexpensive and effective. General advertising in newspapers or on radio for students will sometimes elicit inquiries regarding employment. It would not seem wise to spend much money in this way for staff recruitment because the target audience of the periodical is much too general. Further, in this broad approach to the announcement of vacancies, one is likely to receive inquiries from persons lacking qualifications to teach in Christian schools.

Reporting vacancies to school board members, to parents and pastors through regular newsletters, and to fellow principals can often bring inquiries or names of possible candidates. This kind of sharing also becomes a call to the school community to join in prayer for the selection of staff members.

Application form. Each school will want to develop an application form that meets its own needs. Information about the candidate should include personal data (name, address, telephone number, date of birth, marital status), educational data (high schools and colleges attended and dates, major and minor fields, degrees earned), work experience data (places of employment listed chronologically), and spiritual commitments and theological understandings (see exhibits A and B).

Interview. Although the principal is the interviewer, the interview actually is carried on two-directionally. The interviewee is evaluating the principal and the school he represents, and deciding whether or not he really wants to submit an application. The principal must recognize that in this type of interview he is "on the spot" and is being evaluated as he is also evaluating the job-seeker.

In most instances the recruitment interview will not be the

selection or employment interview. It will frequently be conducted on a college campus and is used to find candidates with whom one can carry forward the selection process. The principal should prepare for the interview by:

1. Setting a clear purpose for the interview
2. Having materials on hand to distribute to the interviewee
3. Being aware of time limitations
4. Formulating leading questions and determining topics to be covered
5. Having an outline on which to jot notes during the interview
6. Seeking the Lord's guidance for his words and his manner.

Before the interview is closed, the candidate should be told the deadline for submitting the application, the selection procedures involved, and when he will hear further regarding the application.

Placement agencies. In addition to the very helpful college placement offices, there are various other placement services available. Christian schools will find little help from general commercial agencies because it is impossible to know if candidates are Christians. Organizations of Christian schools sometimes provide useful listings of teacher candidates for a small fee to the candidate as a part of the services provided member schools.

References and examinations. Reports about academic competence, teaching skills, and personal qualities including Christian commitment are generally available as a part of the placement credentials at the Christian college. The small size of most of these institutions makes it possible for the interviewer to obtain personal comments from the one in charge of the placement office or from the members of the education faculty. These persons will often be helpful in the recruitment process by encouraging candidates to apply to schools that they know and consider suitable for the candidate.

Examinations are seldom used in recruitment. If National Teacher Examination scores are available, they should be considered but not emphasized. The use of situational questions for candidate response (oral or written) can be helpful in evaluating the insight that is so important in teaching. The doctrinal que'stionnaire generally used in some form by Christian schools is an essential "examination" tool.

Recruitment Calendar

Because the field of candidates for Christian school positions is much more limited than for public schools, recruitment starts early in the year in order to have a staff by early summer for the fall opening. The following can be thought of as an ideal calendar:

December 1	– Written survey of staff to determine tentative plans for next school year
January-February	– Announcements of known vacancies and college recruitment visits
February-March	– Collection of data on candidates and beginning of selection process
March-April	– Renewal of contracts and offer of contracts to selected candidates

Evaluation of Recruitment Program

The principal and the school board need to evaluate the recruitment program periodically to determine its effectiveness and make warranted modifications. Answers should be sought to questions such as these:

How much was spent each year for recruitment? What was the average cost of recruiting each teacher (total recruitment cost divided by number of teachers employed)?

What institution(s) supplied most of the staff? Were others contacted?

What factors caused applicants employed to be interested in this school?

Was a recruitment calendar developed and followed? Did recruitment efforts begin soon enough?

To what extent were various recruitment factors utilized?

Were recruitment factors used that brought no return for several successive years?

What long- or short-term factors in recruitment were insufficiently used?

EXHIBIT A

Application for a Professional Position

FASTEN RECENT

PHOTOGRAPH

HERE

Mr.
Mrs.
Miss _____

| Last | First | Middle | Maiden | Spouse's first |

Present Address _____ Telephone _____ Area Code_____

_____ Zip Code _____

Permanent Address _____ Telephone _____ Area Code_____

_____ Zip Code _____

Social Security Number _____ Are you a citizen of the United States? yes ____ no _____

Date of Birth _____ Birthplace (state) _____ Height _____ Weight _____
            Month   Day   Year

Physical handicaps and condition of health during the last two years _____

_____

Marital Status: ☐ Single ☐ Married ☐ Widowed ☐ Divorced ☐ Separated

No. of children_____ Their ages_____

Church Membership _____ Location_____

Name of Pastor _____ Address _____

Organizations to which you belong _____

Present Salary _____ Minimum salary you will accept _____

What grades to you prefer? _____

List in order the three subjects you feel best qualified to teach _____

_____   _____

What extra curricular activities do you feel capable of directing?_____

_____

Teaching certificate held: State_____ Type_____ Date of issue_____

EXHIBIT A *(Continued)*

EDUCATIONAL BACKGROUND

HIGH SCHOOL

School _____ Location _____ Year of graduation _____

UNDERGRADUATE COLLEGES AND UNIVERSITIES

	Name of Institution	Location	Dates Attended	Degree Mo. Yr.
REGULAR SESSIONS			19__to 19__No. Yrs.____	
			19__to 19__No. Yrs.____	
SUMMER SESSIONS			19__No. sem. hrs. ____	
			19__No. sem. hrs. ____	
EXTENSIONS			19__to 19__No. sem. hours____	
			19__to 19__No. sem. hours____	

College Major_____ No. sem. hours_____ College Minor_____ No. Sem. Hours_____

Number of semester hours in professional education courses_____

SUPERVISED STUDENT TEACHING

Inclusive Dates Mo. Yr. to Mo. Yr.	Name of School	Place	Grade	Subject

GRADUATE COLLEGES AND UNIVERSITIES

	Name of Institution	Location	Dates Attended	Degree Mo. Yr.
REGULAR SESSIONS			19__to 19__No. Yrs. ___	
			19__to 19__No. Yrs. ___	
SUMMER SESSIONS			19__No. sem. hrs. ____	
			19__No. sem. hrs. ___	
EXTENSIONS			19__to 19__No. sem. hours_____	
			19__to 19__No. sem. hours_____	

REGULAR TEACHING EXPERIENCE

List all experience chronologically. Indicate part-time teaching by an asterisk. Do not include substitute teaching.

Inclusive Dates Mo. Yr. to Mo. Yr.	No. Years	Name of School	Location City State	Public or Private	Grade	Subject

EXHIBIT A *(Continued)*

OTHER EMPLOYMENT

List chronologically all non-teaching work experience:

Inclusive Dates Mo. Yr. to Mo. Yr.		Kind of work	Employer and Address

(Enclose sheet with additional listings of any above items if necessary.)

Dates of military or alternative service:_____ to _____

If alternative service, where did you serve?_____

REFERENCES

List the names of three persons who know of your work professionally or of your qualifications for teaching. (Examples: Superintendent or principals with whom you have worked in recent years, the teacher with whom student teaching was done, the college supervisor of student teaching, and college professors in your major and minor fields and in education.)

Name	Position	Present Address

Are you registered with a college placement officer or a teacher's agency? _____

Please ask above to have your confidential placement credentials sent to this school.

Why are you applying for a position with this school? _____

_____

When and why did you leave your last position? _____

_____

Have you ever been dismissed or asked to resign from a teaching position?

Yes _____ No _____ (If yes, give details on a separate sheet.)

Have you ever been arrested for other than a minor traffic violation?

Yes _____ No _____ (If yes, give details on a separate sheet.)

When can you take a position if appointed?_____

Are you under contract at the time of making this application? _____ for the ensuing year? _____

What is the latest date by which you may resign without violating your contract?_____

I affirm that my statements and answers on this application are correct to the best of my knowledge.

Signature _____ Date _____

EXHIBIT A *(Continued)*

STATEMENTS OF
CHRISTIAN FAITH AND COMMITMENTS

1. Write a spiritual autobiography and attach to this form. Your autobiography should include your personal relationship to Christ, your present relationship to the church, and your philosophy of Christian life and commitment.

2. State your present thinking on the following items (write concise answers and attach them to this form according to the outline):

   A. State your views on the inspiration and authority of the Scriptures. How does God reveal Himself to man?

   B. State what you believe about the person and work of Christ including the virgin birth, His deity, the bodily resurrection, and second coming.

   C. State your understanding of the person of the Holy Spirit and describe His work in the life of an individual.

   D. What is your belief about the Genesis account of the creation? The fall of man and its results?

   E. What is your understanding of the gospel teaching regarding church-state relationships, allegiance to government, and the use of force?

   F. What is your understanding of Christian ordinances?

   G. What are your positions regarding social drinking, dancing, movie going, gambling, and wearing of jewelry?

3. What is your conviction regarding the Christian school and the distinctive characteristics of its educational practice?

4. Are you prepared to lead a young person to faith in Christ as Saviour and Lord?

5. If you are married, does your wife/husband give sympathetic support to the views you have expressed on this application?

6. Are you willing to be guided by the sponsoring board of trustees, the cooperating Mennonite conferences, supporting Mennonite congregations, and the administration of the school? Are you open to consider changes in behavior that would make your work more acceptable to these groups?

7. Comments:

EXHIBIT B

DAYTON CHRISTIAN SCHOOLS, INC.
325 Homewood Avenue
Dayton, Ohio 45405

ATTACH
RECENT
PHOTO

APPOINTMENT QUESTIONNAIRE

Date_____

Name _____

Present Address _____

City_____ State _____ Zip _____ Phone (area code)_____

Permanent Address _____

City_____ State_____ Zip_____ Phone (area code)_____

Position Desired _____

I. PERSONAL BACKGROUND

Date of Birth _____ Height_____ Weight_____

Physical Disabilities _____ If Yes, describe _____

Military Status _____Years of Military Service _____

Social Security Number_____ Citizenship _____

Marital Status: Single ☐   Married ☐   Widowed ☐   Divorced ☐   Divorced and Remarried ☐

Spouse (Name and Age) _____

Children (Name and Age)   _____

_____   _____

_____   _____

II. EDUCATION*

A. Name & Location of School Include High School, College, Graduate Work, and summer sessions in order taken	Dates	Time Spent	Semester Hours Credit	Degree or Diploma (B.S., M.A. etc.)	MAJOR SUB. and Semester Hours Credit	MINOR SUB. and Semester Hours Credit

B. Bible Training: Credits Earned

  1. Bible and Theology   _____

     Christian Education   _____

  2. Other formal or informal Bible training_____

  3. Do you personally study the Bible consistently?_____

  4. List and describe any courses taken in Christian philosophy of education and/or courses giving specific training for Christian day schools.

_____

C. General Data:

  1. What courses in the teaching of reading have you taken? (K-7 only)_____

_____

  2. What teaching certificates do you hold?_____

  3. What plans do you have for further training?_____

*Enclose an unofficial transcript or an accurate listing of the college courses taken, credits and grades earned.

III. TEACHING EXPERIENCE

Grade and/or Subjects	School	Address	Principal	Year(s)

Practice Teaching: School_____ Grade level or subject _____

Amount of experience_____ Grade received _____

Comments_____

_____

Other work experience:_____

Present employment and address_____

Why do you desire to make a change from your present position?_____

Present salary: _____

IV. POSITION DESIRED

Grade Level

Rate preferences as
1st, 2nd, 3rd

K	1	2	3	4	5	6	7	8	9	10	11	12

Subject Preference: 1st Choice   2nd Choice   3rd Choice

_____   _____   _____

What experience have you had in working with the age level you desire to teach?

_____

Are you interested in an administrative position now or in the future? (Please specify) _____

How do you feel about teaching a Bible class on your preferred level? _____

Are you interested in or do you have training or experience in any of the following?

____ Sports (specify)   ____ newspaper   ____ student government
_____   ____ photography   ____ art
                          ____ debate   ____ library
____ Music (specify)   ____ drama   ____ office work
_____   ____ Gospel team   ____ other (specify)
____ Yearbook   _____

When could you begin work here? _____

V. PERSONAL VIEW

1. How long have you had assurance that Christ is your personal Lord and Saviour?_____

2. Describe your present relationship with the Lord. _____

3. Denominational preference _____
   Church presently attending_____

4. Church activities involved in (please indicate degree of regularity) _____

   _____

5. State what you consider to be the important function of the Christian day school and the distinctive characteristics of its educational practice. _____

   _____

6. Do you accept the biblical account of creation of the world and man as recorded in Genesis?_____

7. Please share with us your personal attitude as a Christian toward liquor, tobacco, and matters of recreation and entertainment. _____

8. If married, will your wife (or husband) give sympathetic support to these same standards of faith and life?_____

9. Have you recognized any leading of the Lord in your life toward Christian school teaching? _____
   If so, describe _____

10. As a teacher in a Christian school, on what basis would you require obedience of your pupils? _____

11. What do you understand to be the proper relation of a teacher to the moral and spiritual lives of his students? _____

12. Are you prepared to lead a young person to accept Christ as his personal Saviour? _____

13. Have you been involved in personal evangelism? _____

VI. REFERENCES

1. Spiritual—A spiritual leader who knows you well:

   Name _____ Address _____

2. Pastoral—Pastor of the church you are now attending (if different from above).

   Name _____ Address _____

3. Professional—Someone who has supervised your work, preferably in education.

   Name _____ Address _____

4. Friend—A person who has known you for a number of years (not a relative).

   Name _____ Address _____

STATEMENT OF FAITH

1. I believe the Bible to be the inspired and the only infallible authoritative Word of God.

2. I believe that there is one God, eternally existent in three persons: Father, Son and Holy Spirit.

3. I believe in the deity of our Lord Jesus Christ, in His virgin birth, in His sinless life, in His miracles, in His vicarious and atoning death through His shed blood, in His bodily resurrection, in His ascension to the right hand of the Father, and in His personal return in power and glory.

4. I believe that man is sinful by nature and that regeneration by the Holy Spirit is essential for his salvation.

5. I believe in the continuing ministry of the Holy Spirit, by whose indwelling the Christian is enabled to live a godly life.

6. I believe in the resurrection of both the saved and the lost, they who are saved unto eternal life and they who are lost unto eternal damnation.

7. I believe in the spiritual unity of believers in our Lord Jesus Christ.

8. I believe in the creation of man by the direct act of God.

Dayton Christian Schools neither support nor endorse the World Council of Churches, National Council of Churches or any other world, national, or regional organization which gives Christian recognition to unbelievers or which advocate multi-faith union.

Signature:_____

PLEASE RESPOND TO THE FOLLOWING
SITUATIONS AS IF YOU ARE INVOLVED:

1. Parents are to pick their children up at the school at 6 p.m. following a field trip. By 6:30 one child is still left. No one answers the phone at his home. What do you do? _____

2. A student with a bitter spirit tries to disrupt class with small mutterings and movements. When you give him attention, he quiets down; but the next day he does the same. What do you do? _____

3. Some girls come to you with complaints about an unfair action by another teacher. If their claims are true, the other teacher is doing some serious harm. What do you do? _____

4. Your class has expected a test on Monday. On Friday, some strong-willed students group together and try to pressure you to postpone the test until Wednesday. What do you do? _____

5. A fellow teacher starts to fill you in on the past mistakes of the principal (or another teacher). What do you do? _____

6. You receive a student's paper with an obscene phrase written at the top. The student says he didn't write it himself—that it was written by another student who graded the paper. What do you do? _____

7. Your class has looked forward all week to having a film on Friday. Just before classtime, you find that the only available projector had been broken that morning. How do you tell the class? And what do you do that period?_____

"The LORD said to Gideon, 'You have too many men for me to deliver Midian into their hands. In order that Israel may not boast against me that her own strength has saved her, announce now to the people, "Anyone who trembles with fear may turn back and leave Mount Gilead."' So twenty-two thousand men left, while ten thousand remained.

"But the LORD said to Gideon, 'There are still too many men. Take them down to the water, and I will sift them for you there. If I say, "This one shall go with you," he shall go; but if I say, "This one shall not go with you," he shall not go.'

"So Gideon took the men down to the water. There the LORD told him, 'Separate those who lap the water with their tongues like a dog from those who kneel down to drink.' Three hundred men lapped with their hands to their mouths. All the rest got down on their knees to drink.

"The LORD said to Gideon, 'With the three hundred men that lapped I will save you and give the Midianites into your hands. Let all the other men go, each to his own place'" (Judges 7:2-7).

"As Jesus went on from there, he saw a man named Matthew sitting at the tax collector's booth. 'Follow me,' he told him, and Matthew got up and followed him" (Matt. 9:9).

"One of those days Jesus went out into the hills to pray, and spent the night praying to God. When morning came, he called his disciples to him and chose twelve of them, whom he also designated apostles . . ." (Luke 6:12-13).

"While they were worshiping the Lord and fasting, the Holy Spirit said, 'Set apart for me Barnabas and Saul for the work to which I have called them'" (Acts 13:2).

3. Selection

The most important job of the principal is to recommend to the board a quality staff. In general, the school will succeed or fail on the merits of its personnel.

It should be clear that the board itself is not directly involved in staff selection except as noted in the following quotation from Willard S. Elsbree and E. Edmund Reutter, Jr.:

> A board of education should limit its participation in teacher selection to the formulation of policies and, when filling vacancies, to passing on the specific recommentations of the superintendent of schools. School board members should not interview candidates nor spend hours of time trying to interpret the credentials of individual teacher applicants. The only exception to this principle is when a board of education is choosing a new superintendent of schools. The job of discovering talent and appraising the qualifications of applicants is a professional task which falls wholly within the province of the superintendent of schools. He may delegate some of this responsibility, but the board should hold him accountable for results. If the superintendent is not capable of selecting competent personnel he should be replaced. But under no circumstances should the board of education assume the function of teacher selection.[1]

Know What You Want

Not just anyone is a suitable candidate for the staff of a Christian school. Nor is just any sincere Christian suitable. In the recruitment and selection process it is necessary for the principal (1) to have a clearly articulated statement of the goals of the school and (2) to determine the kind of person who is needed to help achieve these goals. A job description for each vacancy will further clarify the traits and competencies that are needed in each position.

Search Diligently and Carefully

Effective personnel selection is preceded by good recruitment policies and practices. It is based on a wide search for the best candidates available. Although it may be difficult to choose among several well-qualified persons, one will always be glad he searched diligently as the months and years go by. The temporary anxiety of the decision-making process will yield to the long-term satisfaction and joy of seeing an effective and cooperative staff member serving in the school at God's call. While it is true that God many times overrules for good our mistakes and carelessness, it is also true that He sometimes needs to teach us lessons we seem unable to learn except through suffering the consequences of our impatience.

Proper selection is also carried out by assessments based on the most complete collection of data possible about all candidates.

Application forms (see chapter 2, exhibits A and B). All information requested on an employment application should be useful either in the selection process or after the individual is hired. The information should be considered carefully in determining the fitness of the candidate for the job. If a coaching assignment is part of a science teacher's job description, the candidate's statements regarding extracurricular activities he could direct become important information. The applicant's sex may be a qualifying factor if it is important to achieve or maintain a balance of men and women on the staff. Responses to doctrinal questions will be a factor in the screening process. The principal may want to take each application and on the basis of its contents (including neatness and language usage) rank the candidates.

References (see exhibits A and B). The appraisals of a candidate by those qualified to evaluate his personality, Christian graces, and professional competence are significant and should be attended to carefully. Unfortunately, one must note that pastors' evaluations are frequently discounted by educators because they are often vague and more complimentary than warranted.

The Buckley Amendment as passed by the United States Congress has tended to make writers of evaluations hesitant to point up weaknesses. An evaluation form that notes that the candidate has waived his rights to see the contents assures one of a more honest appraisal. An experienced principal also learns to interpret statements that a novice may take at face value: "With additional growth Mr. Brown should become a good teacher" translates into "Mr. Brown is now below average; taking him is a risk." "Miss Jones grew in her understanding of child nature" means that she really does not understand children very well.

Because of the reticence of many people today to write a statement of honest evaluation, one can often get a more candid opinion by using the telephone. A long-distance telephone toll of several dollars is a small price to pay for a clear person-to-person evaluation. A telephone call is often useful in clarifying an ambiguous statement on a reference form or in understanding what seems to be a puzzling contradiction.

Judgments of colleagues. In schools that are large enough to have department heads or several persons in administrative positions, principals should involve these heads in the selection process. They can read and evaluate applications, recommendations, and credentials. They can interview the candidate separately or with the principal. To make their contacts less formal, such persons can give the recruit a tour of the school grounds while engaging him in relevant conversation. The sharing of findings will assure more responsible decision making. Furthermore, the involved colleagues will grow as professionals in the Christian school and have their morale strengthened. "In the multitude of counsellors there is safety" (Prov. 11:14 KJV).

Appraisal of credentials. Many teacher education institutions go to much work to prepare sets of confidential materials to help principals select teachers. Such credentials generally include lists of college courses taken or unofficial academic records, evaluations by major instructors and student teaching supervisors, employment records, and personal data. These folders are of great help in evaluating candidates.

Be wary of any credentials, including transcripts, carried by a candidate.

Observation on the job. Evaluation of a skill such as teaching is done best by observing actual performance. Talking about teaching is never the same as doing. For this reason student teachers who do well are often employed by the school that hosted them. Unfortunately, it is difficult for a principal to have the opportunity of an on-the-job observation. Some have asked candidates to prepare a lesson to present in class when they come to the school for an interview. The contrived nature of this arrangement makes its value dubious at best and completely unnerving to the candidate at worst.

Health. The physical and emotional health of candidates needs to be considered in making the final selection. Normally this will be indicated in the responses on the application form or, more likely, on recommendations from professional sources. People with emotional health problems are often hesitant to admit to them because of the repeated rejection the information may cause. Examinations of a psychological nature are seldom warranted if the principal is alert and checks out suspicious signals.

Persons with physical handicaps should be given fair consideration in relation to nonhandicapped persons. Depending on the handicap and the climate of the school, a teacher with a handicap may be completely successful in the teaching situation.

Written examinations. Written examinations are seldom more than moderately helpful in selecting teachers. If scores are available from tests such as the National Teacher Examination, they should be utilized. When working with the small population available as teacher candidates in Christian schools, principals will find such examinations of less value in discriminating than more subjective devices.

The only truly useful kind of an examination might be a locally developed situation-type test in which the candidate describes how he would handle a problem situation described on paper (see chapter 2, exhibit B). Such situation-response devices can also be used orally in the interview.

Interviews. The selection interview is used to narrow the field of candidates to one person who will be offered a contract. This interview can be conducted by the principal alone or with several colleagues. In many Christian schools a committee of the board assists the principal in conducting the last interview. It is a time of making final evaluations of the person's attitudes, love of the Lord, respect for others, love of teaching, understandings of Christian school philosophy, and competence for teaching. An unhurried hour is usually needed for a valuable interview. Normally the board members will not be involved in interviewing a person until the principal has put him in priority positions one or two as qualified to fill the vacancy. The principal recruits and selects candidates; the board says yes or no to his recommendations or helps decide between candidates in particularly difficult cases.

The considerate principal will recognize that a candidate comes to the interview situation with a great deal of anxiety. He will therefore make sure to clarify in advance the time and place of meeting with directions for getting there. When aware of the candidate's arrival, he will meet him warmly in the outer office and take him to his own office or other place of interview. He will help him feel relaxed and, if the interview is with board members, will introduce them by clearly enunciated names and personal information. At the close of the interview, he will explain when the decision of the board regarding employment will be made. Audible prayer for God's guidance should occur sometime during the interview.

Questions asked in the interview should be very specific. If the interviewer has before him an outline of topics to be covered, he can gather a goodly amount of information in a short time. Exhibits C, D, and E list suggested questions that will help one know a candidate and his qualifications.

Practice Christian Courtesy

Candidates generally have applications pending at several schools. They may also have their own ranked listings of preferred schools. In fairness to the candidates the Christian school principal will clarify with each one the selection procedures and notification timetable. Having this information will give them needed feelings of security. It will also enable them to make satisfactory decisions regarding their choices. The principal will also strictly adhere to the schedule he outlines. If there are unavoidable delays, he will keep the candidates informed as soon as possible.

If he knows there is little or no likelihood that a particular candidate will be employed, he will convey this information kindly and directly. It is unfair to have a candidate thinking he is being seriously considered when he is not.

It is gracious and right to inform the successful and the unsuccessful candidates. It is not always easy to tell a good prospect that someone else was chosen, but there is no alternative for a fair-minded principal.

A principal should practice fairness in treating confidential information with care. Doing so would include the avoidance of any discussion about the qualifications of a candidate with any other candidate.

Be Alert

A principal should be alert for the constant job changer. Occasionally there are valid reasons for changing employment after a year or two. But all candidates with such experience records should be questioned carefully; their responses should be verified by their former employers.

If a candidate does not want his present employer to know he is applying, this is a signal for great caution. In some circumstances this request is reasonable: too early in the current year; fear of bad relationship with present employer; fear of publicity. However, in many circumstances granting this request spells trouble because one of the most important references is closed off. If such a request is made, the candidate should be asked to give his reasons and to state an approximate date when the employer may be contacted. The hiring principal will then need to decide if he is willing to abide by the timetable. Obviously, his present judgment as to the desirability of employing the candidate will largely determine whether or not he accepts the condition imposed.

Before, during, and after every aspect of the selection process, one must pray. God will hear and guide, and prayer will also make the principal more open to receive wisdom and guidance.

Even though school may be about to open, one must never panic into hiring a second-best person. In a quiet and confident faith one remembers that God is far more concerned about the school than any principal could ever be. One trusts God to provide a staff that is of highest quality spiritually and professionally.

EXHIBIT A

Delaware County Christian School

Malin Road
Newtown Square, Pennsylvania 19073
215/353-6522

*The fear of the Lord is
the beginning of knowledge.
Proverbs 1:7*

Dear

_____ has applied to the Delaware County Christian for a position on our faculty. ____ has given us your name as a reference.

Would you please give us your confidential evaluation of the candidate's manner of life, ability to get along with others, adaptability, personality, intelligence, appearance, and success in the teaching profession? Thank you.

Your prompt reply will be much appreciated. A self-addressed, stamped envelope is enclosed for your convenience.

Sincerely yours,

Roy W. Lowrie Jr.

Roy W. Lowrie, Jr.
Headmaster
RWL:ih
Encl.

EXHIBIT B

educating the total person
Dayton Christian Schools, Inc.
325 Homewood Ave., Dayton, Ohio 45405 ● Phone: 513/278-9645

Re:

Dear

The individual named above has made application for a teaching position with Dayton Christian Schools, Inc.

We are seeking your advice concerning this person's ability and character; but we desire to obtain only information which is in keeping with the Lord's principles as found in Matthew 18:15. Therefore, please do not share any faults or negative thoughts about this person if you have not counselled them regarding this deficiency.

Your insights and comments are warmly welcomed.

In Christ's service,

Claude E. Schindler, Jr.,
Superintendent

CES/cn

Enclosures: Referral Form &
Return Envelope

"In Christ are hidden all the treasures of wisdom and knowledge." Colossians 2:3

DAYTON CHRISTIAN SCHOOLS, INC.

325 Homewood Avenue
Dayton, Ohio 45405

STAFF EMPLOYMENT REFERRAL FORM - S/E

Name of Applicant _____ Date _____

Position Applied For_____ Your Phone No. ___/_____

Which of the following spiritual gifts do you see in the applicant? Which one would be primary?

Teaching   Exhortation   Administration

What are some positive qualities about the applicant which show a calling to teaching or administration? What qualities show a genuine love for children?

What are some of the qualities and actions of the applicant which show spiritual maturity?

What areas of professional performance have you had to speak to this individual concerning the fact that he/she was not meeting your expectations?

What grade level and/or subject matter do you feel the applicant is best suited for?

Is the applicant able to communicate effectively and command the respect of students, parents, fellow staff members?

Have you seen a genuine servant spirit in the applicant?

How long have you known the applicant?

Signed_____ Position _____

—Please use the reverse side for any additional pertinent comments—

EXHIBIT C

Interview Questions by Categories

Reliability

What are your reasons for applying here?

What were your reasons for leaving your present job?

Other than regular classroom duties, what responsibilities did you assume? For how long?

Have you ever been forced from a job? Why?

Have you ever quit a job? Why?

How long do you plan to live here and continue teaching?

Initiative

What type faculty committees would you like to serve on?

What professional organizations do you belong to? What do you think of them?

What are your feelings toward mandatory teacher attendance at extra-class activities?

What student organizations would you like to help with? Not work with?

What experience have you had involving children in activities other than those in your classroom?

When were you last in college? Workshops? Seminars?

Willingness to Work

When did you have your first job?

What was it? What did you do?

How long did you stay? Why did you quit?

Did you work during college? How many hours weekly?

Did you work as a child?

Aptitudes

What do you feel would be your most difficult task concerning this job? Why?

What do you see as your greatest asset in teaching?

You know you have certain weaknesses as a teacher. What are they?

What makes teaching enjoyable for you?

What type student do you think you best relate to? Least?

Educational Method

Do you prefer "tracking" or heterogeneous grouping?

How do you intend to individualize instruction in a heterogeneous group?

What textbooks or series of texts do you prefer? Why?

Did you recommend any curricular changes or suggest innovations in the school in which you last taught?

Emotional Stability

If a child said you were unfair, what would you do?

If a parent said you were unfair, what would you do?

How will you react to the student who challenges your authority in class?

Human Relationships

If you had to name the one thing that helped students like you, what would it be? Teachers? Parents? Administrators?

If you could change your personality one way to help you get along better with people, what would you change?

Ever live in dorm/fraternity/sorority in college? What did you like about it? Dislike?

What are some personality characteristics you find undesirable in people?

Discipline

Do you feel classroom control will be a problem for you? Why? Why not?

Do you feel discipline outside your classroom—halls, assemblies, and so forth—is your responsibility? Why? How will you accomplish this?

Who should be responsible for the discipline in your school?

When should you send a student to the office?

What is your attitude toward individual versus total class punishment?

What do you consider to be the proper classroom atmosphere for learning?

What rules did you have for your classroom?

Salary

How much do you think a teacher should make?

Do you know approximately how much you would make here? How do you feel about our salary and you?

Do you think you should be paid for lunch duty, playground, club sponsorship? How much?

Does your husband or wife work? Where?

From "Interviewing Teacher Candidates," Supplement to *The Master Teacher* (Manhattan, Kansas, c. 1973).

EXHIBIT D

Christian School Interview Questions

1. How did you become a Christian?
2. What training have you had in Bible?
3. Do you know how to lead a student to Christ?
4. Have you ever led a person to Christ?
5. Have you taught Sunday school or a Bible club?
6. Have you worked in a Christian camp?
7. What Christian work have you done?

8. Do you believe that God has given you the spiritual gift of teaching?
9. What is your church background and present membership?
10. Do you agree to the school's Statement of Faith without reservation?
11. Do you hold any unusual doctrines not included in the school's Statement of Faith?
12. What are the basic differences between the Christian and a secular school?
13. Why do you feel led of God to teach in a Christian school?
14. What are your convictions on the use of wine, liquor, tobacco, drugs and entertainment?
15. Are you looking for a Christian school in which to invest your life, or one where you can get experience to prepare for another job?
16. What is your view of the inspiration of the Bible?
17. What is your view of the creation of man?

Adapted from James W. Braley, editor, *Manual of Administration for New and Young Christian Schools* (n. p.: California Association of Christian Schools and National Christian School Education Association, 1974), "Recruiting and Screening Teacher Applicants," p. 6.

EXHIBIT E

Interview Questions — Dayton Christian Schools, Inc.

1. Tell us about your family.
2. Why do you want to teach in a Christian school? Is it a conviction or a preference?
3. How do you respond to authority?
4. What do you feel is your strength as a teacher?
5. What do you feel is your weakness as a teacher?
6. If single, what does your father think of your teaching in a Christian school?
7. In all humility what do you like about yourself?
8. What do you dislike about yourself?
9. If single, what do you think about marriage—about a life of singleness?
10. Where do you place parents in your role as a teacher?
11. What have you learned recently about the Word of God?
12. Are you in debt?
13. When do you think a student should be sent to the office for discipline?
14. Can you foresee some problems that may arise in a Christian school but would not in a public school?

15. Do you see Christian education as a conviction or a preference for Christian parents?
16. What do you believe your spiritual gift to be?
17. If you were to employ yourself, what help would you need?
18. How would you teach a particular subject differently in a Christian school than in a public school?

"Make known to them the design of the temple—its arrangement, its exits and entrances—its whole design and all its regulations and laws. Write these down before them so that they may be faithful to its design and follow all its regulations" (Ezek. 43:11).

"Now when he saw the crowds, he went up on a mountainside and sat down. His disciples came to him, and he began to teach them . . ." (Matt. 5:1-2).

"When he was alone, the Twelve and the others around him asked about the parables. He told them, 'The secret of the kingdom of God has been given to you. But to those on the outside everything is said in parables' " (Mark 4:10-11).

"I have been reminded of your sincere faith, which first lived in your grandmother Lois and in your mother Eunice, and, I am persuaded, now lives in you also. For this reason I remind you to fan into flame the gift of God, which is in you through the laying on of my hands" (2 Tim. 1:5-6).

4. Orientation

First impressions are usually lasting impressions. The kind of orientation school leaders give to newly employed staff members may well determine the feelings of contentment or disappointment of those persons for months or even years. Although the Lord enables people to rise above disappointing induction experiences and to forgive those who failed, in our humanity we find that these thoughts tend to linger in our minds. An induction program should be planned, considerate, and personal.

Communication

The process of communication between school and employee actually begins with the preemployment experiences of recruitment and selection. As noted in the previous chapter, the person-oriented principal keeps candidates fully informed of their status. He promptly notifies the successful candidate of his being elected to the staff.

Now there are new needs for communication. What housing is available? When does the contract year begin? What classes/grades are assigned? What textbooks/resources are available? How can friends be found?

Personal letters and mimeographed staff bulletins should go out to the newly employed staff members as these needs develop. It is helpful if the principal anticipates needs and answers questions before the employee asks them. This is the time, if not before, to give a personal copy of the faculty handbook.

Contract

As a first part of the communication process, the principal offers the successful candidate a written contract of employment. A few schools still rely on oral contracts or a simple written statement that the candidate has been hired. Such arrangements are unsatisfactory because they frequently lead to misunderstandings regarding conditions of employment. A young teacher confided to a professional visitor that she understood her salary was to be a certain figure but when she received her first check it was obviously less than the amount she had expected. This misunderstanding was the basis of the dissatisfaction that led to her resignation at the end of the year. Unfortunately, the school board never knew of the real reason for her leaving because she was too timid to broach the subject with them. A written contract would have made this a much happier situation.

A contract is an agreement between two parties. It is an acknowledgement by the employee that he understands the conditions of employment and is committing himself to fulfill them. It is a pledge by the employer to reimburse the employee for his services at a stipulated rate so long as the conditions are not violated.

Vaguely worded contracts are almost useless. Specific salary figures, schedule of payments, and specific fringe benefits should be included in the body of the contract or appended thereto. Likewise the dates of the contractual period are important. Unusual and general obligations should be stated. On the other hand, not every duty of a contracting employee can possibly be listed. It is to be understood that certain usual duties such as playground supervision and collecting milk money are appropriate jobs to be assigned to teachers though not specifically noted.

To provide a just measure of security to employees in schools not providing tenure, it is desirable to use a continuing contract, that is, to state that the contract will be renewed automatically for an additional year unless discontinued for stipulated reasons by either party by a certain date (see exhibits A, B, and C).

Provision of Textbooks

Teachers appreciate being provided in early summer with all the textbooks and curriculum guides they will be using during the school year. These materials provide the opportunity to develop lesson plans in advance and to outline in tentative form the year's work. In one school a beginning teacher seemed to some of his colleagues unusually nonchalant about daily planning. It soon became clear that he could be so because he had made his lesson plans during the summer for at least six weeks in advance. Even with planning, few new teachers can be so relaxed, but such advance work does indeed decrease the level of anxiety that to some extent plagues all beginners.

Housing Assistance

Whether single or married the new employee will have housing needs. He will need particular assistance if he is not familiar with the community and/or does not have family or friends living in the area. The principal should keep a file of available housing, particularly names of landlords with rental units. Frequently, owners are eager to rent to school personnel because they know they will make good tenants. Sometimes members of the Christian school family will make economical housing available as a part of their commitment to Christian education. For teachers who prefer to buy housing immediately, it is helpful to work with a real estate broker who has a special interest in the school and understands the financial situation of Christian school teachers.

Housing assistance is one of the principal's tasks that can rather easily be delegated. The school secretary, the business manager, a board member, or a school volunteer can give personal attention to those who have housing needs.

Preschool Conference

Some orientation needs are very personal and individual and are best taken care of on a one-to-one basis. Some needs are general and are most efficiently met in group settings. In addition, group settings meet social needs of staff and help effect a team spirit of working together.

Preschool conferences are generally held the week before pupils report for classes. The length of the conferences may vary from one day to one week or even longer. The optimum length would seem to be two days with an additional half day for orientation of new teachers only. It is important that this session be the first part of the conference so the novices can feel a bit at home before the oldsters take over the school! Time for individual work in classrooms is an essential part of preschool conferences.

Topics to be covered for the benefit of beginning personnel include payroll arrangements, requisitioning of supplies, personnel policies, and school forms and routines. In short, it is a good time to cover all school procedures that do not need to be brought to the attention of continuing staff. In addition to procedures, some time should be spent on Christian school philosophy. Assigning each new teacher the reading of a book like Frank E. Gaebelein's *The Pattern of God's Truth* is most worthwhile. If the assignment is made when the teacher is hired, the book could be the basis of an hour of good discussion in the orientation conference.

Introduction to Community Services

Moving to a new community always brings a certain amount of trauma, especially to families. Where shall we go to church? How shall we find a physician, a dentist, an eye doctor? Which bank is best? Where does one find best buys in groceries, housewares, furniture? Where is a reputable automobile mechanic? What about finding babysitters?

In some way suggestions that will be helpful in answering these questions need to be given. They should be offered before, during, and after moving—when the need is present. They can be answered personally by the principal, a staff volunteer, or by an up-to-date mimeographed list of such services.

Faculty Handbook

A faculty handbook is essential in every school. It should contain all the routines, forms, and policies that affect the daily work of the staff. It should be indexed and continually updated. A good way of expediting such updating is by using a looseleaf notebook with topics organized by a numerical system. Exhibit D lists the table of contents for the handbook at Lancaster Mennonite High School.

Buddy System

Some schools have used with good results a buddy system to orient new staff to school and community. The principal assigns a returning teacher to a new teacher on the basis of assumed compatibility and asks the veteran to begin a personal relationship before school opens and to continue it throughout the year. If the buddies are selected well, a beautiful, open relationship can develop between the two people. A new teacher will often feel free to ask "insignificant" but bothersome questions of a fellow teacher that he feels would be a nuisance to take to the principal.

Supervision

An important aspect of the induction process that becomes a part of the in-service program for all teachers is supervision by the principal. Supervision takes many forms; its purpose is always to enable the teacher to improve the quality of classroom instruction. Observing the teacher and then conferring about the observed experience should happen in the first several weeks of school. A thoughtful principal will ask the beginning teacher to tell him in advance of a lesson that he would like observed. Supervisory visits to new teachers should be by prearrangement the first month or two.

Another helpful supervisory practice is to arrange for the beginning teacher to have occasional opportunities to observe excellent teachers for a class period or a half day. Persons observed can be teachers within the same school or nearby.

Assistance in planning should be offered to the new teacher. Frequently, the opportunity is presented when the principal stops by the teacher's room after school with a "How was your day?" kind of question. There should be many occasions to talk informally. In this way the teacher becomes more free to share his problems with the principal before they become unbearably heavy. On the other hand, the principal needs to avoid monopolizing a teacher's time that he needs to use for planning.

New teachers need a great deal of commendation. They are not sure how well they are doing, and a sincere word of appreciation helps immeasurably.

Praying together is a way of building Christian brotherhood and freeing the Holy Spirit to minister strength and wisdom to those who share in the Christian school ministry. The considerate principal will not push a new teacher to lead in prayer before he is comfortable doing so.

New Teacher Assignments

Teachers with seniority sometimes feel they have earned the right to have first choice of class and extracurricular assignments. "Rights" are often nothing more than selfishness in masquerade. Principals and teachers in the Christian school will try to give beginning teachers the lightest loads, the most cooperative groups, and the fewest extra assignments. The success and happiness of the neophyte professional is a high-ranked goal of all his colleagues.

EXHIBIT A

DAYTON CHRISTIAN SCHOOLS, INC.
TEACHER'S CONTRACT

The School Board of Directors appoints you _____ as _____ teacher in the Dayton Christian Schools. Date of employment shall be from _____ to _____. Remuneration for this period of employment will be $_____. The school will provide fringe benefits as outlined in the attached schedule. Said teacher agrees to abide by the following criteria:

(Please initial each item after reading.)

1. Your duties will involve not only the responsibilities ordinarily incumbent, but also those responsibilities related to the special spiritual ministry to which you are called—the training of the child in Christian faith and practices. In a very real sense, therefore, it is the expectation of this Board that you will strive at all times to understand, appreciate, and love the pupils entrusted to you for instruction, and that you will, to the best of your ability, provide for their fullest intellectual,

physical, emotional, and spiritual development. As a servant of the Lord Jesus Christ, you will *faithfully attend* the regular services of your church as an example of the believer.

2. The teacher affirms that, as part of the qualifications for employment, he/she is a "born again" Christian who knows the Lord Jesus Christ as Saviour and Lord (John 3:3; 1 Peter 1:23).

3. The teacher agrees to be present on time for faculty devotions, which begin each school day, and to remain in the building thirty (30) minutes after classes have been dismissed. The teacher also agrees to remain after school for such meetings and conferences as may be called by the principal or other administrative officers acting in his behalf.

4. The teacher agrees to abide by the regulations set forth in the Faculty Handbook and to cooperate in every way with the school authorities. The teacher will maintain a quiet, dignified, well-disciplined, and studious classroom, study hall, or work group.

5. The teacher agrees to accept his or her proportionate amount of supervision outside of regular classroom assignment, the extent of such supervision and assignment to be determined by the principal of the school.

6. The teacher will present certification from a reputable physician showing that he or she has passed a physical examination, including a tuberculin test. State requirements on such TB tests include the following: (1) Initial employment requires TB Tine test *or* chest X-ray, depending on medical history. (b) After three years, a repeat skin test is required, and documented proof placed in employee's file. (c) If chest X-ray is medically indicated, it should be followed up annually. (d) All "positive" TB skin-test reactors need chest X-ray.

7. This contract becomes valid upon the filing of the proper teacher's certificate for the State of Ohio in the superintendent's office.

8. A copy of the complete college transcript will be filed in the superintendent's office five (5) days prior to the first day of teaching.

9. The teacher agrees to accept, without reservation (be it mental or verbal), the attached Educational Philosophy of Dayton Christian Schools. (Please initial each Statement of the Philosophy, indicating your acceptance.)

10. The teacher accepts, without reservation (be it mental or verbal), the attached Statement of Faith, and has initialed each statement.

11. The teacher has read the attached Job Description, and agrees to abide by the requirements listed.

12. The teacher will avoid highly debatable topics as much as possible, especially as they relate to denominational issues.

13. The teacher agrees to adhere to 1 Corinthians 3:16-17 and 6:19-20. We interpret this to mean abstinence in drinking, smoking, and in the use of profane language. The teacher also agrees that the roles of the male and female are clearly defined in 1 Corinthians 11:3. Romans 1:24-32 states that God recognized homosexuals and other deviates as perverted, and because of this willful condition such cannot be an employee of this school.

14. The teacher agrees to follow the biblical pattern of Matthew 18:15-17 and Galatians 6:1, and always give a good report. All differences are to be resolved by utilizing biblical principles—always presenting a united front.

15. The teacher agrees to go through the three-year ACSI In-Service training program for Christian school teachers. Any book already read or tape already listened to will not have to be repeated in order to fulfill the requirements of the program.

16. Because the work wherein we are engaged is an area involving the religious tenets of belief and is composed of spiritual activities over an educational function, and that it is a sacred undertaking, we cannot authorize anything other than an arbitration before the believers for any kind of dispute that may exist. Arbitration in this manner is the only biblical means which is acceptable for discipline purposes. Parties signing this document waive all rights to take their cause before a court of law. First Corinthians 6:1-8 is very clear on this point and, as believers, we are to obey these instructions.

17. The contract between teacher and Dayton Christian Schools can be voided when any of the above requirements are violated by either party, or for any deviation on scriptural grounds. If, after signing the contract, the teacher desires to be excused from said contract, a written request must be made to the superintendent who will in turn present it to the board for consideration.

18. This contract must be returned by the teacher within twenty (20) days following its receipt.

Entered into this _____ day of _____

_____   _____
Teacher   Chairman, Dayton Christian Schools, Inc.

                                 _____
                                 Superintendent

THE EDUCATIONAL PHILOSOPHY OF THE DAYTON CHRISTIAN SCHOOLS

(Please initial each paragraph)

The educational philosophy of Dayton Christian Schools is based on a God-centered view of truth and man as presented in the Bible. Since God created and sustains all things through His Son, Jesus Christ, the universe and all life are dynamically related to God and have the purpose of glorifying Him. This is pointedly true of man who was made in God's image, different in kind from all other creation, with the unique capacity to know and respond to God personally and voluntarily. Because man is a sinner by nature and choice, however, he cannot, in this condition, know or honor God in his life. He can do this only by being born again through receiving Jesus Christ as Saviour and Lord, and thus be enabled to do God's will, which is the ultimate purpose of his life.

The entire process of education is seen as a means used by the Holy Spirit to bring the student into fellowship with God, to help him become strong or mighty in the spirit, to assist him in developing a Christian mind, to enable him to think God's thoughts, to train him in Christlikeness, to teach him to act like God and to help the student demonstrate Christlike character qualities so that he can fulfill God's total purpose for his life personally and vocationally. He is taught the Bible so he may understand God as well as his own true nature and function as God's image. He is developed and related to God as a whole person, that is: spiritually, mentally, physically, and socially. He is taught to see all truth as God's truth and to integrate it with, and interpret it by, God's Word. He is educated as an individual with his own unique abilities and personality who learns to live and work with others at home, in the church and in a changing secular society. He interacts with and is taught by parent and teacher models who are _____ themselves born again and have this perspective on life.

The authority for such an education comes both from God's command that children be taught to love God and place Him first in their lives and from the fact that parents are responsible for the total education and training of their children. At the parents' request, the Christian school, along with the church, becomes a partner in giving this education. The Christian school is an extension of the local evangelical fundamental church's Christian education program, serving the parent in fulfilling their responsibility of educating the child. From this philosophy stem certain aims _____ and objectives:

I. For the spiritual and moral growth of the students, the school seeks:
1. To teach the Bible as God's inspired Word and to develop attitudes of love and respect toward it.
2. To teach the basic doctrines of the Bible, that is: God, Jesus Christ, Holy Spirit, Man, Salvation, Church, Scriptures, Satan, Angels.
3. To lead the pupil to a decision of confessing Christ as Saviour and Lord.
4. To develop a desire to know and obey the will of God as revealed in the Scriptures.
5. To equip the student to carry out the will of God daily.
6. To impart an understanding of each Christian's place in the church and its worldwide task of witnessing, evangelizing and discipling, and to stimulate the student's involvement in this task.
7. To develop the mind of Christ toward godliness and sin and to teach the students how to overcome sin.
8. To encourage the development of self-discipline and responsibility in the student based on respect for and submission to God and all other authority.

9. To help the student develop for himself a Christian world view by integrating life and studies with the Bible.

II. For the students' personal and social development, the school aims:
1. To help the student develop his personality based on a proper understanding and acceptance of himself as a unique individual created in the image of God and on the fullest possible development of his own capabilities.
2. To teach the students to treat everyone with love and respect as unique individuals made in God's image.
3. To make the student a contributing member of his society who realizes his dependence on others and their dependence on him and the need to serve them.
4. To promote an understanding of time as a God-given commodity and the individual's responsibility for effective use of time.
5. To show a realistic and biblical view of life and work, and provide skills for personal relationships and future endeavors.
6. To develop both good and proper attitudes toward marriage and the family and also the understanding of skills needed to establish God-honoring homes.
7. To promote physical fitness, good health habits, and wise use of the body as the temple of God.
8. To impart the biblical attitudes toward material things and to encourage individual responsibility of using them for God's glory.
9. To engender an appreciation of the fine arts through the development of the student's understanding and personal expression.

III. Academically, the school endeavors:
1. To promote high academic standards within the potential of the individual as uniquely created by God and to help the student realize his full academic potential.
2. To help each student gain a thorough comprehension and command of the fundamental processes used in communicating and dealing with others, such as reading, writing, speaking, listening, and mathematics.
3. To teach and encourage the use of good study habits.
4. To teach the student how to do independent research and to reason logically.

5. To motivate the student to pursue independent study in areas of personal interest.
6. To develop creative and critical thinking and the proper use of biblical criteria for evaluation.
7. To promote good citizenship through developing the understanding and appreciation of our Christian and American heritages of responsible freedom, human dignity, and acceptance of authority.
8. To discuss current affairs in all fields and relate them to God's plan for man.
9. To produce an understanding and appreciation for God's world, an awareness of man's role in his environment, and his God-given responsibilities to use and preserve them properly.

IV. Working with the homes from which the students come, the school desires:
1. To bring those whom we find that are not Christians to the saving knowledge of Jesus Christ.
2. To aid families in Christian growth and to help them develop Christ-centered homes.
3. To cooperate closely as servants to the parents in every phase of the student's development, especially as it relates to the school program.
4. To help the parents to understand the school's purpose and program.
5. To assist parents in keeping up with the changing culture and its effect on the home and the implications for their children.
6. To encourage regular attendance and involvement in the local church.
7. To encourage parents to realize and shoulder their responsibility for the spiritual, moral, and social education of their children.

DAYTON CHRISTIAN SCHOOLS, INC.
STATEMENT OF FAITH

(Please initial each item)

1. I believe the Bible to be the inspired and the only infallible
——— authoritative Word of God.

2. I believe that there is one God, eternally existent in three persons: Father, Son, and Holy Spirit.

3. I believe in the deity of our Lord Jesus Christ, in His virgin birth, in His sinless life, in His miracles, in His vicarious and atoning death through His shed blood, in His bodily resurrection, in His ascension to the right hand of the Father, and in His personal return in power and glory.

4. I believe that man is sinful by nature and that regeneration by the Holy Spirit is essential for his salvation.

5. I believe in the continuing ministry of the Holy Spirit, by whose indwelling the Christian is enabled to live a godly life.

6. I believe in the resurrection of both the saved and the lost, they who are saved unto eternal life and they who are lost unto eternal damnation.

7. I believe in the spiritual unity of believers in our Lord Jesus Christ.

8. I believe in the creation of man by the direct act of God.

Dayton Christian Schools neither supports nor endorses the World Council of Churches; National Council of Churches; nor any other world, national, or regional organization which gives Christian recognition to unbelievers, or which advocates multi-faith union.

_____

Date

_____

Signed

EXHIBIT B

LANCASTER MENNONITE CONFERENCE SCHOOLS
ANNUAL PROFESSIONAL EMPLOYEE CONTRACT

It is agreed by and between _____ ,
the professional employee, and the Board of Trustees of the Lancaster Mennonite Conference Schools, the employer, that said employee shall, under the authority of said board, and subject to the supervision and authority of the properly authorized administrator, serve as _____
_____ at _____

for a term of _____ days during the _____ school term for an annual compensation of $_____ payable every two weeks from September through August. Deductions shall be made as required by law or for loss of time or for any other reasons as agreed upon by and between said employee and the Board of Trustees.

It is further agreed that this contract shall be renewed for another year not less than sixty calendar days before June 30 of the current contractual term, unless the employee voluntarily wishes to terminate the contract because he finds the conditions of the contract unsatisfactory or for other valid reason, or unless the employee has been rated unsatisfactory by his chief administrator or by the Religious Welfare Committee of the Lancaster Mennonite Conference Schools or because through decreased enrollment, difficult economic conditions, or change in organizational structure the employee's services are no longer needed.

It is further agreed that this contract may be terminated by the employer without prior notice in case of immorality, overt disloyalty to the position of the Lancaster Mennonite Conference, or extreme incompetency. In all cases of termination or non-renewal of contract by the employer, the employee shall be granted the right of appeal according to policies adopted by said Board of Trustees.

It is further agreed that faculty members will be asked to accept non-teaching responsibilities such as study hall, cafeteria, detention, and general campus supervision; the enforcement of all aspects of the conduct codes; the participation in professional duties out of school hours; and that the administration will seek as far as possible to achieve equity in all staff assignments.

It is further agreed by both parties that they shall commit themselves wholeheartedly to the promotion of an effective Christian education program, to seek to live in full obedience to the will of God, and to maintain a vital life in Christ through the Holy Spirit by prayer, Bible study, and sharing of their faith with others.

In witness whereof, the parties hereto have affixed their signatures this _____ day of _____ , 19___ .

_____   _____
President   Secretary

                                        _____
                                        Employee

EXHIBIT C

NORFOLK CHRISTIAN SCHOOLS
FACULTY AND STAFF CONTRACT

Believing that God has led in this decision, the Executive Board of the Norfolk Christian Schools has appointed _____ as _____ in the Norfolk Christian Schools. The following agreement is the basis for this contract. Date of employment shall be from _____ to _____ and shall include the faculty and staff work days in the approved school calendar.

Remuneration for the period of employment will be $_____ to be paid as follows:

1. To be applied toward Norfolk Christian Schools
   Tuition . . . . $_____
2. To be paid (biweekly) (monthly) through
   payroll . . . . $_____
3. Other . . . . $_____

Normal tax and social security deductions will be made from this salary. In its effort to be the channel through which God supplies the needs of those who minister at Norfolk Christian Schools, the school has been enabled, under God, to provide other material, educational and service benefits in addition to salary. These benefits entitled "Norfolk Christian Schools Co-worker Benefits" are set forth in the faculty handbook.

It is understood that all faculty and staff members will be subject to whatever provisions the executive board may make for supervision of the work within the authority structure of the schools. In loyalty to the schools and to preserve the unity of the work, they will bring any questions and criticisms directly to the administration. In signing this contract you hereby signify your agreement with the following statement:

I acknowledge Jesus Christ as my Lord and Saviour and declare my agreement with the doctrinal basis and purpose of the Norfolk Christian Schools as expressed in the Bylaws and with the stipulations of Article IX of the Bylaws.

I further undertake as God shall give me strength, to endeavor to live in full obedience to God's will as it is set forth in the Scriptures, forsaking all ungodliness and worldly lusts, walking in that

holiness and temperance which will be an example to the youth
and adorn the doctrine of our Lord and Saviour Jesus Christ, and
fellowshipping with other Christians in a local church.

Witness the following signatures this _____ day of
_____ , 19 _____ .

_____
President, Norfolk Christian Schools

_____
Superintendent

_____
Faculty or Staff Member

EXHIBIT D

FACULTY HANDBOOK
LANCASTER MENNONITE HIGH SCHOOL

Table of Contents

"Do not take advantage of a hired man who is poor and needy, whether he is a brother Israelite or an alien living in one of your towns. Pay him his wages each day before sunset, because he is poor and is counting on it. Otherwise he may cry to the LORD against you, and you will be guilty of sin" (Deut. 24:14-15).

"One man gives freely, yet gains even more; another withholds unduly, but comes to poverty" (Prov. 11:24).

"You are to use accurate scales, an accurate ephah and an accurate bath" (Ezek. 45:10).

"But seek first his kingdom and his righteousness, and all these things will be given to you as well" (Matt. 6:33).

"Then some soldiers asked him, 'And what should we do?' He replied, 'Don't extort money and don't accuse people falsely—be content with your pay' " (Luke 3:14).

"Masters, provide your slaves with what is right and fair, because you know that you also have a Master in heaven" (Col. 4:1).

5. Compensation—Salaries

When Jesus sent out the 70 disciples on their evangelistic mission, He told them to accept the material support offered them "for the worker deserves his wages" (Luke 10:7). In Romans 15:27 the Apostle Paul points out that there is a close relationship between spiritual blessings and material blessings. That is, those who perform a spiritual ministry should be supported in material ways.

Boards of Christian schools are concerned about a spiritual ministry, but they need to compensate those who perform this ministry with reasonable financial support. It is good to trust the Lord for the wages that will need to be paid, knowing that God indeed is faithful. However, it is foolhardy and "sub-Christian" to build a school ("tower"—Luke 14:28) without adequate resources to operate it. Withholding payroll checks may occasionally be necessary, but it will rarely happen if the board members are committed to living just as sacrificially as they expect their staff members to do.

A just compensation for employees is necessary if the school is to prosper. A just compensation enables the employees to give full attention to their work. In the earlier years of the Christian school movement a former foreign missionary who was teaching in a Christian school wept as he shared with a colleague his problem in being able to carry adequately the financial burden of a teen-age family. The emotional anxiety interfered with his being effective in teaching preparation and presentation. Either the mission board under which he had served or the Christian school board under which he was presently serving was remiss in giving him a just compensation for his labors.

Financial sacrifices are made by almost every teacher who serves God in the Christian school. That is not unfair. But it is unfair if the remuneration is grossly inadequate for his needs, and it is unfair if the school employees are making a disproportionate share of the sacrifice for the school. Many teachers are deeply committed to Christian education, but only the grace of God keeps them faithful to that commitment when parents and students have access to money for a living style far beyond the means of the teachers.

Every Christian school board needs clear and updated salary policies. One of the principal's tasks is to keep before the board the financial needs of the staff and ways the school can more adequately and justly meet those needs. When teachers need to "moonlight" to support their families, their salaries are unjustly low.

What Is a Fair Salary?

Cost of living. A fair salary takes into account the cost of living in a given community. Although this cannot be determined with complete accuracy and it varies from one family to another, a general estimate is possible. A survey of community housing and food costs (the big factors that are also variable) added to an estimate of clothing, transportation, health, and miscellaneous expenses will give a helpful picture of living costs. In addition, the salary should permit savings toward large purchases such as car and home, and toward retirement.

The cost of living is increasing at an unprecedented rate currently with no improvement in sight. Christian schools must keep this rise in mind in the annual setting of salaries. Unless foresight is used, salary increases will lag behind the rise in cost of living. It must be recognized that a psychological presumption exists in the minds of all that makes a dollar-amount seem like a great salary improvement although it may not be an improvement at all when viewed as a percentage increase and compared with the increase in the Consumer Price Index.

Prevailing salaries. Each community differs not only in cost of living but in style of living. As professionals, Christian school teachers identify with the total professional community, especially in the area of teaching. For this reason, some Christian schools tie their salary schedules to the local public school salary schedules. They set their salaries at, for example, 85 percent of the area public school salaries. The disadvantage of using such a ratio as a final determinant of salaries is that it makes one factor dominate and presupposes the validity of the salary level of the public schools.

Ability to pay. Some schools are able to pay higher salaries than others for a variety of reasons. Some are saddled with large capital costs; others obtain adequate facilities for a small outlay of dollars. Some parent groups are high on conviction for Christian education but low in financial resources. In some cases a few parents carry a conviction not shared by the larger Christian community.

Productivity. The standard of living achieved in the Western world has been accomplished in large measure by increasing the output of goods in a constant period of working time. Productivity in schools can be increased by enlarged class size so that each teacher produces more "scholars" in the same time period. Increased productivity can also be seen in the extra-class duties a teacher carries so that fewer employees are needed than otherwise.

Increased productivity is hard to come by in education. Most Christians schools are already getting maximum production out of their teachers; some teachers are overproducing because of the value they place on hard work and their conviction for Christian education. Each school should seek to give teachers optimum work loads (most efficient, long-term level) rather than maximum loads (constant highest possible performance). Nevertheless, ways should be found to reward those who are more productive than others.

Morale. Salary levels are important in determining staff morale—important but not all-important. If one or several teachers are struggling to "make ends meet," and commiserating with one another in the faculty lounge, their discouragement tends to infect the entire staff and to encourage dissatisfaction and bitterness. The principal needs to stay sensitive to the financial struggles of his colleagues. He will strengthen their morale by being an example of Christian stewardship, by recommending to the board that considerate salary adjustments be made when possible, and by modeling a deep sense of dependence on God and trust in His ability to supply His children's needs according to His sovereign will.

Influence on recruitment. As the principal carries out his staff recruitment contacts, he becomes aware that his school's salary policies affect his recruitment success. Apart from the intervention of God's Spirit who may put it into a candidate's heart to accept the position regardless of salary, the school that offers an unjust salary will not be able to attract quality personnel. Instead, it will find itself staffed, if at all, by those who were passed over in the screening processes of other schools.

Long-term commitments. Salary policies need to be fair to the new recruit and to the staff veteran. Education salary patterns in the United States tend to reward seniority rather than productivity or need. Christian schools need to bring the ethics of Jesus to bear on this issue.

Frequently seniority and need are close companions. A young college graduate may feel he is earning quite enough on a typical Christian school salary. He marries; his wife is working, but he is surprised that the costs of housekeeping and a few "pleasures" take so much of their combined income. Pregnancy brings an end to his wife's earnings at the same time that their living costs escalate. Suddenly, he realizes that his adequate Christian school salary of his single years is grossly inadequate. Later, when he has teen-age children and then college students, his living costs continue to increase. If the school has salary policies that reward him according to experience, training, and need, he will no doubt stay with the school. If the policies do not so reward him, he will reluctantly choose a less fulfilling but more lucrative job.

Other Salary Considerations

Credit for prior experiences. Not every recruit is a recent college graduate getting his first teaching experience. Desirable candidates may have had few or many years of teaching in other Christian or secular schools. How much is that experience worth to the prospective new employer? Each school needs a policy to guide the principal in making salary offers to such persons. Except in unusual circumstances such persons will not accept a position that does not recognize financially their past experience. On the other hand, it may not be just to others serving in that school to give an experienced person full credit for each year taught elsewhere. One possibility is to give full credit for previous experience in a similar setting but only half credit for teaching in situations that have less professional transfer value: foreign experience, public school experience, or experience at a different level— elementary, secondary, collegiate.

The school also needs to establish whether credit shall be given for prior non-teaching experiences. Travel, pastorate, and certain other types of background experience are the most frequently rewarded.

Extra pay for extra duties (see exhibit A). Some staff members are asked to perform duties outside of the regular school day. Examples are coaching, play directing, yearbook and newspaper advising, choral ministries in churches. A typical approach is to pay a lump sum to the teacher who accepts one of these responsibilities. Determining the amount of such extra pay requires wisdom that it, too, will be a just figure. A danger in Christian schools is that unqualified or overworked persons will accept these duties in order to increase a bare-bones salary.

Another approach is to decrease the teaching load in some proportionate manner for teachers carrying these outside-of-school-day duties. This method has advantages but may not be completely just if the hours the teachers are required to be at school are not reduced.

Merit pay. Merit pay has been proposed for many years but has failed to gain acceptance in schools. The reason is that the measurement of merit is so completely subjective. Teachers do not want to be measured by a merit yardstick that they do not understand in advance. Principals are uncomfortable recommending for merit increments if they cannot clearly defend the rationale for selection.

Better than a vague merit pay policy would be a program

that identifies involvement beyond the call of duty and rewards those who voluntarily and willingly make themselves available for such activities.

Annual increments. According to some clearly outlined schedule, teachers should know that their earnings year by year will increase because of their experience. One's salary can hardly increase annually by $500 (apart from cost-of-living increase) for 20 or 30 years. No school could afford to pay such salaries; neither do other salary guidelines justify such a spread between beginning and retiring teachers' salaries. However, such increases may be feasible annually for 10 or 15 years and occasionally thereafter.

Single salary schedule (see exhibit B). In recent years the single salary schedule has become popular on the American educational scene. It has won favor because it is easy to administer and makes for better relationships among faculty members by eliminating jockeying for competitive salary increases. The single salary schedule provides equivalent pay for equivalent work based on the factors of preparation and experience. All classroom teaching positions are assumed to be equivalent work regardless of level—elementary or secondary.

There are disadvantages to the single salary schedule. It does not differentiate on the basis of need or of merit. The need factor can be applied to a single salary schedule by dependency increments, or such like, to the teacher's regular position on the schedule. Despite disadvantages, the single salary schedule seems currently the best approach to salaries because teachers feel more comfortable and positive where it is used. They understand fully how salaries are determined; this nearly eliminates the temptation to distrust those who establish salaries.

Index schedules (see exhibits C and D). Juggling dollar amounts annually on a single salary schedule so that veteran teachers do not get a proportionately smaller piece of the salary pie is time consuming and difficult. The index salary schedule achieves a greater degree of justice with less effort. In the index schedule an index figure or multiplier replaces a dollar amount at every level determining preparation and experience. Thus, all positions on the scale are expressed in ratios with the beginning position (bachelor's degree, no experience) being the base (1.00). Once an index schedule is adopted, only the base salary figure needs annual adjustment because all other salaries automatically adjust themselves proportionately.

One concern with index scales is that in high periods of inflation the indexes need periodic adjusting to avoid the broadening of the range between beginning salaries and salaries at the top of the scale.

Collective bargaining. Collective bargaining assumes two parties with antagonistic interests who need to be forced to compromise a settlement somewhat balanced between their opposing desires. In recent years nearly all public schools have had to adopt this procedure for setting salaries and fringe benefits.

Collective bargaining does not seem to be an appropriate way for brothers and sisters in Christian schools to solve wage problems. Bargaining negotiations are costly, time-consuming, and fraught with emotional overtones that can destroy relationships for years. The best way for boards and administrators of Christian schools to avoid these problems is to seek continually the highest interests of all employees and to maintain open channels of communication in hearing their needs.

Administrative salaries (see exhibit E). Many school boards negotiate the principal's salary completely apart from any relationship to what teachers in the school are earning. Other schools find fairness served more satisfactorily by paying the principal what he would receive as a teacher in the school plus a percentage for responsibility. That percentage will vary with school size, amount of responsibility, and the difficulty of the job in that situation. In addition, the principal who is employed during the summer receives a monthly increment prorated from his school-year salary figure.

EXHIBIT A

DAYTON CHRISTIAN SCHOOLS, INC.
Extra Duty and Pay Schedule

GUIDELINES:

A. "Extra Duty," as used in these schedules, refers to those activities which require special work and responsibilities beyond the normal school day and hours, and which are to be performed outside the regular school hours, unless otherwise stated or approved by the superintendent.

B. "Extra Duty" further refers to those professional and other services that are beyond the regular duties that are due the school by reason of the employee's regular contract.

C. Persons employed in administrative status or in a non-classroom assignment are not usually eligible for stipends.

D. The local building administration of the "extra duty" program shall be the province of the principal. Assignments in each building program shall be recommended by the principal to the superintendent.

E. Stipends for positions may be divided between two or more persons when deemed necessary.

F. Volunteer parents will not receive pay.

G. Combined girls and boys sport under the same coach, and if both teams play in an approved league or schedule=highest stipend plus one-half of other.

H. The foregoing list of duties and remunerations takes into consideration such factors as special preparation, general public relations value, pressure from crowds, injury/safety concerns, nights out, number of people involved, revenue produced, individual development versus team coordination, number of appearances, training of other associates, span of leadership-control-supervision, budgeting involvement, equipment control, regulations to keep abreast of, total number of hours, and so forth.

I. Each person is expected to do all his work from the heart as to the Lord, "ready unto every good work." It is also hoped that each person envisions his work as a ministry, not just a job!

ACADEMIC AND STUDENT LEADERSHIP:

Department heads $200.00
Yearbook Sponsor 450.00

Newspaper Sponsor 100.00
Student Council Sponsor 200.00
Christian Service Sponsor 150.00

ATHLETIC ACTIVITIES:

Director of Athletics (1 additional
   free period) $350.00
Assistant Director of Athletics 150.00
Varsity Coach—Basketball 650.00
Varsity Coach—Soccer 600.00
Varsity Coach—Baseball and Softball 450.00
Varsity Coach—Track 600.00
Varsity Coach—Cross-country 350.00
Varsity Coach—Volleyball. 350.00
Varsity Coach—Wrestling 350.00
Varsity Coach—Tennis 200.00
JV Coach—Basketball 375.00*
JV Coach—Soccer 325.00
JV Coach—Track 250.00*
Jr. High Coach (7-8)—Soccer 300.00
Jr. High Coach (7-9)—Basketball 300.00
Elementary Coach 150.00
Varsity, JV Cheerleaders 250.00
Cheerleader Advisor Head 50.00
Jr. High Cheerleaders (7-9) 175.00
Drill Team 200.00
Jr. High Track (7-8) 300.00
Jr. High Cross-country (7-8) 200.00*

MUSICAL AND DRAMA ACTIVITIES:

Pep Band (all home athletic events) $175.00
Brass Ensemble (10 performances
   minimum) 275.00
Choral Ensemble (15 performances
   minimum) 350.00
Gospel Drama Team (5 performances
   minimum) 350.00
Fall Drama (1 production per year) 275.00
Spring Musical (1 production per year) . . .   350.00

If in conjunction with coaching varsity, an additional $100 is added to the varsity rate.

EXHIBIT B

DAYTON CHRISTIAN SCHOOLS, INC.
SALARY SCHEDULE
1978 – 1979

Years of Experience	Bachelor Degree	Bachelor +18 Sem. Hrs.	Master's Degree	Master's +18 Sem. Hrs.	Doctorate
0	$7350.	$7500.	$8150.	$8300.	$9000.
1	7575.	7725.	8375.	8525.	9250.
2	7800.	7950.	8600.	8750.	9500.
3	8025.	8175.	8825.	8975.	9750.
4	8250.	8400.	9050.	9200.	10000.
5	8475.	8625.	9275.	9425.	10250.

6-10 . . . . $250. Increment/Year
11-15 . . . . $275. Increment/Year

ADDITIONAL COMPENSATION:
Head of household with children . . . . $500.
Head of household with no children (includes singles) 250.
Family with working spouse (full time) . . . .   0.

Experience in Christian school counts full. Experience in public school teaching, up to fifteen (15) years, to be given at 3/4 credit of DCS salary scale.

EXHIBIT C

NORFOLK CHRISTIAN SCHOOLS
SALARY SCALES

I. FACULTY: All faculty are paid according to a basic scale with supplements for those having dependents or additional responsibility. To find the proper classification, match the column which shows the teacher's professional preparation and the line showing years of experience. For salary purpose a half year counts as a whole year. Multiply the factor listing by the Annual Salary Factor to get the basic salary.

Annual Salary Factor:_____

Professional Preparation

Yrs.		Bachelors	B.A. ± 9 hrs. toward MA	B.A. ± 18 hrs. toward MA	Masters	Masters ±30	Doctors
E	0	.88	.90	.92	.94	.97	1.00
X	1	.90	.92	.94	.97	1.00	1.03
P	2	.91	.93	.95	.98	1.01	1.04
E	3	.92	.94	.96	.99	1.02	1.05
R	4	.93	.95	.97	1.00	1.03	1.06
I	5	.94	.96	.98	1.01	1.04	1.07
E	6	.95	.97	.99	1.02	1.05	1.08
N	7	.96	.98	1.00	1.03	1.06	1.09
C	8	.97	.99	1.01	1.04	1.07	1.10
E	9	.98	1.00	1.02	1.05	1.08	1.11
	10	.99	1.01	1.03	1.06	1.09	1.12

II. DEPENDENT ALLOWANCES for teachers whose primary family income is from NCS: Dependents included are the spouse and dependent children (as defined by IRS). This allowance is based upon a percentage of the Annual Salary Factor as follows:

1 Dependent: 12%   4 Dependents: 26%
2 Dependents: 19%   5 Dependents: 28%
3 Dependents: 23%   6 Dependents: 30%

This supplement shall be known as the Variable Dependent's Allowance (VDA) and shall be added to the basic salary.

III. SALARY REDUCTION: All staff members are given the opportunity to have their salary reduced below scale if they wish to do so for the benefit of NCS. This written request is made when the computation sheet is returned or may be adjusted later as the teacher decides.

EXHIBIT D

LANCASTER MENNONITE HIGH SCHOOL
TEACHER SALARY SCHEDULE – 1979-80

Step	A Bachelor's	B +15 s.h.	C Master's	D +15 s.h.	E +30 s.h.
1	1.00	1.05	1.10	1.15	1.20
2	1.02	1.07	1.12	1.17	1.23
3	1.04	1.09	1.14	1.19	1.26
4	1.06	1.12	1.18	1.23	1.30
5	1.08	1.15	1.22	1.27	1.34
6	1.10	1.18	1.26	1.31	1.38
7	1.12	1.21	1.30	1.35	1.42
8	1.14	1.24	1.34	1.39	1.46
9	1.16	1.27	1.38	1.43	1.50
10	1.18	1.30	1.42	1.47	1.54
11	(15 yrs. exp.)		1.46	1.51	1.58

Schedule Implementation

1. Steps on the salary schedule are not necessarily equal to correspond-ing years of teaching.
2. Advancement on the schedule will generally proceed yearly from step to step upon satisfactory teaching performance.
3. Advancement to classes B through E requires completion of corre-sponding number of graduate credit hours.
4. The Board of Trustees will set the base salary (1.00) annually. For the 1979-80 term it has been set at $9,100.
5. A specific salary is determined by multiplying the appropriate index number times the base salary.
6. Teachers who are on campus each school day for the entire day with teaching and other supervisory responsibilities are classified as full-time teachers. For other persons, the superintendent will determine in cooperation with the teacher, the percentage of teaching and supervisory responsibility being assumed and will determine the salary and benefits in relation to the percentage.

EXHIBIT E

DAYTON CHRISTIAN SCHOOLS, INC.

ADMINISTRATIVE SALARY SCHEDULE
1979 — 1980

The administrator's base salary shall be what he would receive as a teacher with similar education and experience, *plus:*

(1) Compensation for his added responsibilities.
(2) Compensation for time needed for duties in addition to the time needed for a normal teaching load.
(3) Compensation for advanced training in administration.
(4) Compensation for work during the summer.
(5) Compensation for experience in administration.

These guidelines are given as an equitable way to arrive at an administrator's salary. The ranges given are broad enough to allow flexibility, depending on the responsibilities assumed by the administrator. Multiply the teacher schedule by these indexes:

Elementary (up to 250 students) . . . . . . Between 1.20 and 1.30
Elementary (250-500 students) . . . . . . Between 1.25 and 1.40
Elementary (500 plus students) . . . . . . Between 1.30 and 1.50
Secondary (up to 250 students) . . . . . . Between 1.30 and 1.50
Secondary (250-500 students) . . . . Between 1.35 and 1.55
Secondary (500 plus students) . . . . . . Between 1.40 and 1.60
Asst. Principal—Elementary . . . . Between 1.20 and 1.30
Asst. Principal—Secondary . . . . Between 1.20 and 1.30
Business Manager . . . . Between 1.30 and 1.50
Director of Community Affairs . . . . Between 1.30 and 1.50
Superintendent of multiple
    unit system . . . . Between 1.45 and 1.65
(Depending on number of units and number of students.)

"Do not withhold good from those who deserve it, when it is in your power to act" (Prov. 3:27).

"These were his instructions: 'Take nothing for the journey except a staff—no bread, no bag, no money in your belts. Wear sandals but not an extra tunic. Whenever you enter a house, stay there until you leave that town' " (Mark 6:8-10).

"Don't you know that those who work in the temple get their food from the temple, and those who serve at the altar share in what is offered on the altar?" (1 Cor. 9:13).

"Anyone who receives instruction in the word must share all good things with his instructor" (Gal. 6:6).

"The elders who direct the affairs of the church well are worthy of double honor, especially those whose work is preaching and teaching. For the Scripture says, 'Do not muzzle the ox while it is treading out the grain,' and 'The worker deserves his wages' " (1 Tim. 5:17-18).

"The hard-working farmer should be the first to receive a share of the crops" (2 Tim. 2:6).

6. Compensation—Benefits

Personnel or fringe benefits were begun in industry and adopted in education to help make particular job openings more attractive to candidates in a competitive job market. Fringe benefits consist of direct or indirect compensation to personnel without requiring additional services beyond those expected under the basic salary plan. Today these benefits are seen as ways of making an employee's dollar go further or of giving him more pleasant working conditions. Some benefits provide a modified tax shelter for the employee. Compensation dollars seem to stretch for both employer and employee when used for benefits rather than salary. However, employers are finding that benefits are taking an increasing percentage of the compensation dollars, adding hours of bookkeeping time. These benefits tend to receive little recognition because their value is difficult to compute accurately and is easily overlooked in publicity. Nevertheless, fringe benefits are here to stay, and they are important in Christian schools because of the lower salaries that prevail.

Greene states that:

An appropriate benefits program for school employees should be designed to produce conditions of employment conducive to the continual improvement of the instructional program. To accomplish that objective, benefits programs should:
1. Provide security to the individual employee.
2. Safeguard the mental and physical health of the employee.
3. Foster professional growth and morale.
4. Promote staff stability.

A general welfare program should include provisions for leaves of absence, health protection, life insurance, housing assistance, employee counseling, and social and recreational activities.[1]

Table 1 reproduces Castetter's listing of specific types of benefits according to three categories:

Table 1. Types of Collateral Benefits for School Personnel[2]

	Types of Benefits	
Time off with Pay	**Protection**	**Incentive and Improvement**
Vacations	Life insurance	Tuition refunds
Holidays	Health and acci-	Tuition payments
Military	dent insurance	Scholarships
training	Hospital and	Incentive
Personal	medical insurance	increment
absences	Liability insurance	Professional im-
Professional	Retirement	provement credit
absences	Social Security	Noninstructional
Expense	Severance	training programs
allowances	allowances	Expense allowances
		Professional affiliations

Leaves of Absence

A teacher may be granted a leave of absence for a variety of reasons and for short or long periods of time. Board policy should establish types of leaves given and the criteria for approval. The following paragraphs describe the three major groupings.

Sick leave. Sick leave is the most common type of paid leave in education. Considering the dollars spent by the school for sick leave pay, one must conclude that this benefit buys a great deal of security and peace of mind for the employee at relatively low cost.

A common method of providing sick leave is to grant a certain number of days at the beginning of each year to be used as needed. Commonly the range is from five to ten days per year, with ten increasingly being considered a minimum number.

Usually unused sick leave days accumulate year by year to a stated maximum for those continuing with the school. This arrangement provides security against sudden loss of income for the older employee who is most likely to need the benefit. The range of days that may be accumulated is wide indeed; a desirable goal would seem to be 180 days or the number of days in the school year. This is one way of providing disability coverage for a year to the occasional teacher who suffers a prolonged illness.

A number of schools reward teachers who, at termination of employment, have not used all their accumulated sick days. Full remuneration for such days tends to encourage teachers to go to school when they ought to stay home for the health of their students in addition to their own. A more just plan—since using sick days should not be thought of as an unconditional right—is to credit annually each employee with a percentage of his salary for each unused sick day and to make a lump sum payment at termination of employment. It would also seem appropriate to grant such terminal pay only to employees who have served in the school for at least five years.

Personal leave. In recent years some school systems began offering one or two days of emergency leave per year. This soon expanded into personal leave days, and in some cases the number of days increased. When first made available, there were some fears that teachers would misuse the days for shopping expeditions and other activities that would incense the taxpayers. Christian schools that offer personal leave days to teachers will provide guidelines for the use of such days and trust the teachers to use them responsibly. One deterrent to the unnecessary use of personal days is to permit a certain number of sick leave days to be used as personal leave days. Since personal days are generally non-cumulative, their use deducts from the accumulated sick leave reservoir.

Personal leaves of a non-emergency nature can be requested on a form provided by the administration and submitted a week or two in advance. Sometimes the substitute teacher situation coupled with a large number of teacher absences may force the principal to deny a personal leave request.

Professional leave. Schools generally permit teachers to take paid leaves for attending a professional conference or perhaps to visit other schools. Policies may permit one such conference annually by each teacher, or they may limit the number of teachers permitted to go in any one year; in the latter case they rotate those going so that all have the privilege of attending a professional conference over a period of several years.

Year-long unpaid leaves for professional improvement are frequently granted. The improvement may take the form of study, exchange teaching, research, or travel.

Colleges, a fair number of public schools, and a few Christian schools have sabbatical leave policies. After the teacher has been with the school a certain number of years (normally seven to ten), he may submit a professional improvement plan to the administration to encompass one academic year's time. Usually schools pay one half of regular salary for sabbatical leave. A few pay more than this, especially for a study leave. A few also allow a one-semester leave at full salary although this arrangement often makes finding a temporary replacement rather difficult. Persons on sabbatical leave should have their fringe benefits maintained during the year because they are continuing as paid employees of the school.

Following a sabbatical leave, schools assure the employee his former or a comparable position. Service of one to three years following a paid leave is a normal requirement.

Guidelines for approved sabbatical experiences should be published to the faculty (see exhibit A). Decisions regarding the acceptability of proposals should be made on the basis of the anticipated benefit to the school through the improved professional performance of the teacher.

It is this writer's observation that occasional sabbatical leaves are justified by the freshness of new insights and renewed enthusiasm that a faculty member receives from a well-planned year's experience in a different setting.

It should be noted that persons taking extended paid or unpaid leaves of absence should not lose any of their accumulated benefits from prior years. When a person on leave returns, he takes up where he left off; he does not start at the bottom again. For that reason, it is not usually desirable to grant extended unpaid leaves to persons who are not both competent and committed to the school. All such persons should submit resignations and seek reemployment at a later time if they wish to return.

Health and Protection Plans

Teaching is not for those weak in health, physically or emotionally. The intense interpersonal relationships day after day at times drain the energy of the most robust. Teachers should be employed who are in good health; after employment, the principal is concerned to maintain that good health.

Examinations. A physical-mental health examination should be a part of the employing procedures in every school. It can be made by the school physician or by the applicant's own physician. The school should provide a standardized form to be completed by the examiner. To be of most value the report of the examination should be in the principal's hands before school opens. Otherwise, a problem that is uncovered may not be handled without embarrassment.

Frequently, candidates with emotional problems are drawn to teaching. Because of their own experiences, they feel a desire to be involved in the lives of others whom they would help. Such persons must be evaluated carefully; they may make sensitive, caring teachers but only if they have found the strength to cope with their conflicts and find emotional healing. To employ a person with deep emotional problems that are unresolved is to court disaster in the classroom. Principals who do not obtain adequate health records of employees or require health examinations may face difficult situations.

Following employment, periodic physical examinations are important for health maintenance. Every two to four years would seem a reasonable program; perhaps every four years for those under a certain age. Policies of the board may provide for the board to pay a part or all of the costs of these examinations.

Health and hospitalization insurance. This is one of the most important benefits to secure peace of mind to the employee. Health insurance can be obtained through church-related or private organizations. Often national Christian school associations offer health and hospitalization plans at special group rates. Whatever plan is chosen should be "comprehensive" with mental health benefits and lifetime limits on benefits of at least $100,000.

Christian schools can establish policies by which the school and the employee share proportionately the insurance premium or by which the employer pays the full premium. In a similar way, some schools offer coverage for family members at a reduced cost and others pay the total cost of coverage for the immediate family unless otherwise protected.

Some organizations are providing disability coverage for their employees. A Christian college adopted such a plan just days before a relatively young professor was stricken with a long-term disabling illness. Normally, schools provide this coverage through insurance companies; some larger schools provide it through self-insurance by setting aside a reserve fund for such emergencies. The latter generally provide only short-term coverage; others provide it so long as the disability prevents full employment. Social Security provides coverage for certain types of disabilities.

Life insurance. Group life insurance policies are commonly available in business and industry and more recently in education. These policies provide term insurance as a supplement to regular life insurance coverage. As such, they are normally canceled when the employee terminates his services, although they can be converted into higher premium policies.

Retirement. The most widely recognized retirement and disability insurance is provided through the federal government as Social Security. Most workers are covered; however, certain persons may choose to be excluded. Some Christian schools have not chosen coverage, usually for quasi-political reasons.

As a supplement to Social Security benefits most employers provide a pension plan for employees. In some cases nonpublic schools use a commercial plan geared to nonpublic school employees. Some churches have denominational plans.

School personnel need to study and evaluate carefully the various pension plans available, comparing the benefits each provides. Plans are generally financed through obligatory employer contributions and voluntary employee contributions. The employer contribution is normally a fixed percentage of the employee's annual salary.

There are also sheltered annuity plans that school boards can make available to employees. Under such plans personnel may invest part of their salaries in annuities that are not taxed until later when benefits are paid during retirement years. Assuming lower income at that time, one would pay less tax on earnings.

Assistance for Professional Improvement

As a means of encouraging professional improvement and of making a limited amount of money go as far as possible, schools often offer tuition aid for graduate studies. Policies should clearly state the conditions for employees to receive such assistance. The assistance may vary from one-half to full tuition coverage. Sometimes it can be used only at certain colleges. Some place a limitation on the amount that any one employee can receive in a given period of time. It must be remembered that the purpose of such assistance is the improvement of the school in which one is employed.

Frequently, even with tuition assistance, teachers with families are unable to finance graduate studies. In such cases, schools may want to consider setting up a loan fund at low interest to help cover teacher living expenses. A loan of this type can be set up with an accelerating interest schedule to encourage early repayment (see exhibit B).

Some schools have a professional fund of, perhaps, $50 for each faculty member. If he wishes to purchase professional books or magazines, join organizations, or attend conferences, he may submit his expenses for reimbursement to the limit of his allowance. Other schools pay all or a portion of professional conference expenses for their staffs. Frequently, this means that all attend the area Christian schools convention. It may also mean that on a rotating basis a certain number of teachers may be supported each year in attending a conference of their choice.

Another procedure to encourage professional improvement is full or partial payment of dues to one professional organization for each teacher.

Miscellaneous Dollar-Stretching Benefits

Other benefits to make employees' dollars go further include free lunches in the school cafeteria, free or subsidized housing, discounts through school vendors, dental insurance, dependency allowances, tuition assistance for children in the employing school, and credit unions. A recent benefit in view of rising college costs is offering new employees an annual grant toward undergraduate college debts for each year of service to the school (see exhibits C and D for benefits that several schools include with salary schedules).

Tenure

Many states have tenure laws covering public school personnel. Such laws indicate that after a teacher has served a probationary period of several years, he cannot be arbitrarily dismissed. These laws have provided valuable protection for competent teachers, but they have also made it more difficult to terminate the services of the incompetent.

Some independent schools and colleges have developed their own tenure systems. A criticism sometimes voiced is that in spite of tenure, institutions seem to be able to find ways of dismissing those no longer desired. Christian schools can rely on something better than tenure for positive relationships—the trust and caring of Christian brotherhood. To make it work requires a loving, open, listening relationship between staff members, administration, and board.

EXHIBIT A

LANCASTER MENNONITE HIGH SCHOOL

SABBATICAL LEAVE POLICY

1. Sabbatical leaves may be requested after 10 years of full-time service on the Lancaster Mennonite High School faculty, and after every 10 years of such service following a sabbatical leave.

2. Sabbatical leave requests shall be submitted to the principal on a form provided.

3. Only as many sabbatical leaves will be granted in any one year as are judged to be in the best interest of the total school program.

4. Sabbatical leaves will be granted only for study or such activity as can be agreed by the administration and board that will significantly enhance the employee's service to the school.

5. Sabbatical leave activities of an earning nature shall require special clarification.

6. Sabbatical leaves will normally be for one contract year and shall carry a stipend of one-half of the salary the employee would be entitled to for that year.

7. Faculty members on sabbatical leave shall continue to receive all fringe benefits to which they would be entitled if not on leave.

8. A sabbatical leave will be granted with the understanding that the employee will return to full-time service at Lancaster Mennonite High School the following year. Failure to do so will obligate the employee to reimburse the school for his sabbatical salary within 12 months of his notice of termination.

Administrative Timetable

Tentative intent shall be filed with the principal by December 1 of the year preceding the intended leave. Final application shall be filed by March 1.

EXHIBIT B

LANCASTER MENNONITE HIGH SCHOOL

FACULTY PROFESSIONAL LOAN FUND

1. The fund is specifically set up to aid faculty members with educational and living costs while engaged in full-time study either summers or winters.

2. The borrower must agree that he will be returning to the Lancaster Mennonite High School faculty for at least one school year following receipt of loan assistance.

3. Loan applications must be received by May 15 for all loans needed during the following 12 months. Late applications will be considered if money is available provided they are submitted at least 30 days before the funds are needed.

4. The maximum loan available to any one person is $500 unless the fund is not exhausted by applications received by the regular deadline.

5. Interest is due annually on the unpaid balance at the following rates:

> First year 0%
> Second year 3%
> Third year 6%
> Fourth year 9%

6. Repayment of the principal must be made within four years or upon termination of service at Lancaster Mennonite High School, whichever occurs first.

7. All interest received from borrowers will be added to the loan fund to increase the principal available.

8. All funds will be held and administered by the school.

9. Notes are written for one year and are renewable.

EXHIBIT C

DELAWARE COUNTY CHRISTIAN SCHOOL
NEWTOWN SQUARE, PENNSYLVANIA

1979-80 FACULTY SALARY SCHEDULE

Base salary	$8,600
Additional for first dependent	500
second dependent	350
third dependent	300
fourth dependent	250
Master's Degree	300
Master's Degree, plus 30 credits	100
Doctor's Degree	200

Sixth—$100, Eleventh—$150, Sixteenth—$250, Twenty-first—$350, Twenty-sixth—$500 contracts, each

Additional for teaching service, beginning with second year of prior service:

For Prior Service	In D.C.C.S.
$100 per year of service to $1,000 maximum	$180 per year of service, B.A. $230 per year of service, M.A. $250 per year of service, Master's, plus 30 credits $280 per year of service, Doctorate

Merit increases beyond the maximum are not excluded.

FACULTY FRINGE BENEFITS

1. Teachers' children pay 25 percent of tuition and registration. Children must pass the entrance requirements.
2. Seventy-five percent of the teacher's tuition for graduate study in his field.
3. Non-contributory retirement program (T.I.A.A.), 5½ percent of salary upon fourth contract. Teacher may add to this from salary.
4. Group life insurance, equal to twice the teacher's annual salary.
5. Major Medical Health Insurance for the teacher and dependents.
6. Dues for one professional society.
7. Ten days sick leave, cumulative to 30 days, beginning September 1977.
8. Two personal days. Teacher pays substitute.
9. Social Security. Deductions as made against gross earnings, with a like amount contributed by the school.

Important Notice: The salary schedule is subject to change by action of the Board of Trustees. Contracts in force at the time of any change will not be affected until renewed. Contracts are for one school year.

The school is a faith work and all faculty members must share the responsibility with the parents and Society members of looking to the Lord for His provision of all needs (Ps. 62:5).

EXHIBIT D

LANCASTER MENNONITE HIGH SCHOOL

Benefits

1. If faculty member (full-time) is chief family breadwinner, an allowance of $400 for each dependent child under 18 years of age, but not more than three children.

2. Tuition at Lancaster Mennonite High School is provided for children of full-time teachers.
3. Mennonite Aid Hospitalization for each full-time teacher, single or family plan; part-time teachers on a prorated basis.
4. Mennonite Retirement Plan at 5 percent of salary for teachers serving half-time or more.
5. Annual allowance of $50 for professional books, magazines, and so forth.
6. Five annual days sick leave cumulative to thirty; up to three of these days annually may be used for personal leave.
7. Sabbatical leaves under certain conditions.
8. Grants toward payment of pre-employment baccalaureate level college debts.
9. Tuition aid for post-baccalaureate studies according to arrangements negotiated with the superintendent.
10. Free lunches at noon.
11. Disability coverage at 75 percent of salary up to one year.
12. Two hundred dollar deductible family dental coverage at 80 percent level with $650 maximum payment.

Servicing the
School Staff

"Moses inspected the work and saw that they had done it just as the LORD had commanded. So Moses blessed them" (Exod. 39:43).

"Do not pervert justice; do not show partiality to the poor or favoritism to the great, but judge your neighbor fairly. . . .
"Do not use dishonest standards when measuring length, weight or quantity. Use honest scales and honest weights, an honest ephah and an honest hin. I am the LORD your God, who brought you out of Egypt" (Lev. 19:15, 35-36).

"He who listens to a life-giving rebuke will be at home among the wise" (Prov. 15:31).

"Pleasant words are a honeycomb, sweet to the soul and healing to the bones" (Prov. 16:24).

"He who rebukes a man will in the end gain more favor than he who has a flattering tongue" (Prov. 28:23).

"Stop judging by mere appearances, and make a right judgment" (John 7:24).

"Keep a critical eye both upon your own life and on the teaching you give . . . " (1 Tim. 4:16 Phillips).

"Preach the Word; be prepared in season and out of season; correct, rebuke and encourage—with great patience and careful instruction" (2 Tim. 4:2).

"These, then, are the things you should teach. Encourage and rebuke with all authority. Do not let anyone despise you" (Titus 2:15).

7. Evaluation

Evaluation of personnel is a necessary part of all institutions that are seeking to improve. Only that work which is supervised and evaluated improves. Employees desire to have their strengths and weaknesses affirmed because others can often point out that which the person himself is too close to see clearly. But there is also a part of every person that shrinks from looking at his weaknesses in the sight of others, especially of an employer with the power of dismissal. Evaluation must be done, but the principal doing the evaluating must be understanding and clearly concerned for the feelings of the employee. A humble spirit that considers one's own weaknesses is expressive of "the wisdom that comes from heaven . . . pure; then peace loving, considerate, submissive, full of mercy and good fruit, impartial and sincere" (James 3:17).

The purpose of staff evaluation needs to be clearly spelled out so that principal and teacher understand the evaluation from the same point of view. Employees easily see the threat of dismissal in evaluation and employing boards sometimes encourage such fears by their own comments or attitudes.

Purposes of Evaluation

The foremost use of evaluation of job performance is the improvement of instruction. Actually, one is aiming for the improvement of pupil learning, but a principal can gain that end only indirectly, and so he seeks to help the teacher become more effective.

Appraisal is also carried on to identify, reward, and retain those who are serving competently and evidencing growth. Schools having a tenure system use an evaluation process to grant tenure to probationary employees. Finally, a purpose of evaluation is to determine which employees are not successful and evidence so little improvement that they need to be terminated.

Who Is the Evaluator?

The typical pattern is for the immediate supervisor to evaluate the employee. In most Christian schools that person is the chief administrator—also the principal. In schools that are large enough to have elementary/secondary principals or department heads, the responsibility should be shared with them.

Students, especially at the senior high school level, can be involved in the evaluation process. Forms appropriate for their use can be developed within the school or obtained from various sources (see exhibit A). Both teachers and students are more comfortable with unsigned responses. Principals can encourage teachers to share with them the results of student evaluations, but their doing so ought to be voluntary. An understanding principal and a teacher can have a truly helpful conference discussing the results and meaning of such evaluations. Often a teacher needs the strength of a wise supervisor to see the criticisms of students in balanced perspective. Beginning teachers can well be cautioned against reviewing student evaluations at the end of an emotionally draining day. Even hinted suggestions can seem like barbed criticisms to the sensitive beginner.

Perhaps most important is the employee's self-evaluation. Teachers should be encouraged, or required, to complete such forms regularly, more frequently for beginners and less frequently as they gain experience (see Exhibit B). Self-evaluations can also be helpful in principal-teacher conferences and can form the basis of dialogue regarding any differences of perception between the two persons involved. For these conferences it is good for the teacher to use the same form for his self-evaluation as the principal uses for employee evaluation.

Procedures for Evaluation

It should be clear to all employees that regular supervisory evaluations are to be expected. This information can be shared at the beginning of the year at the orientation for new teachers. A statement of evaluation policy and procedures ought to be a part of the faculty handbook along with a copy of the evaluation form that is used. When such procedures are followed, the evaluation process is expected and understood. Teachers feel more secure than they would if evaluation were imposed without warning.

The data base for evaluation should be broad. Teachers often assume that principals do not know anything about their performance apart from a formal classroom visit. They need to be taught that evidence of effectiveness is obtained in a variety of ways; in fact, classroom observation may not be as useful a means of evaluating as many think. Teachers and principals alike must realize that whenever a person who is not a regular part of the group enters a classroom, the classroom atmosphere changes. Usually unconsciously, subtle behavior changes occur in teacher and students. An observer needs to look deeper than surface actions to try to get an understanding of the meaning of what is taking place in the group interchange. Classroom visitation is important but not all important. The principal will also consider quality of written and orally shared plans, out-of-classroom relationships with colleagues and students, professional and spiritual attitudes and growth, cooperation with school goals and procedures, student achievement, and student attitudes outside the classroom.

Conferences need to be scheduled with teachers. These should be relatively frequent with new teachers and occasionally with highly experienced teachers. However, one should not neglect relationships with senior staff members because they also need recognition and encouragement.

Classroom visits should be planned and scheduled so that they do not occur in "hit or miss" fashion. New teachers should be visited by prearrangement at least the first time. In this way they can suggest the lesson they would like the principal to observe. A principal may want to tell the faculty that he is "on call"; he will arrange to visit when they have a special lesson they would like him to share. However, he will also want it to be clear that he will make occasional unannounced visits. If he can visit each teacher at least once a semester, he will do well.

Every classroom observation should be followed by a conference as soon as convenient (see exhibits C and D). This is the place that shared viewpoints regarding the observed events can help the teacher look at himself more objectively. Through the conference the principal can understand more clearly the goals of the teacher and the problems with which he must cope in achieving them. One should accentuate the positive, but avoid being so diplomatic that the teacher never hears the suggestions the principal thought he stated clearly. It is natural to tend to mute one's criticisms because one does not like to hurt another person. The fact of the matter, however, is that genuine caring is confronting when there are errors. For a principal not to call attention to mistakes means that he is not willing to care enough about the person to help him become the best person he can be.

In cases of incompetency that may lead to dismissal or nonrenewal of contract, it is absolutely required that a principal be honest in stating deficiencies. Unless he does so in a way that the employee hears him, the employee has justification for a grievance complaint against the principal.

In addition to the post-observation conference, there should be periodic conferences for the principal to hear the teacher share his planning and his general feeling of achievement in the school. One should draw out the self-evaluation of the teacher. "How do you feel about your teaching?" A good principal knows when to listen and when to make "a word aptly spoken . . ." (Prov. 25:11).

One should have the evaluation report open to the person being evaluated. As one goes over it with him, he should be allowed the privilege of a rebuttal on the record. Both the principal and the teacher should sign the report as evidence that it was shared with the teacher. In some schools a copy of the evaluation is given to the teacher. If not routinely given, a copy should always be available to the employee upon request.

An annual evaluation of each employee should be placed in his file each year before he is offered a contract for the next year (see exhibit E). In addition, copies of periodic classroom evaluations and other pertinent evaluative data should be filed.

Individualize the Evaluation Process

In his conferences with each teacher, the principal should encourage and help him to set his own goals for the year or for an agreed upon period of time. Each one is at a different place in his own awareness of needs and in his professional development. He should be encouraged to work at improvement where he feels the greatest need so long as it furthers the overall goals of the school. Progress in carrying out his improvement plan can furnish the basis for continuing conferences throughout the year.

Evaluation of Administrators

Employees at every level of responsibility are subject to evaluation by those to whom they are accountable. The principal is answerable to the school board; the board needs to have a way of measuring his performance. Although board members may feel incompetent for this evaluation, they can be made to feel more comfortable if they are reminded that he, too, is to be evaluated in terms of the goals that he was expected to meet. They are not expected to evaluate *how* he met the goals, but *how well* he met them. A principal should normally be free to choose his procedures so long as the desired goals are reached. A board that seeks the counsel of the staff before reappointing a principal is wise. Doing so builds bridges of confidence to the employees and helps the board see the principal through the eyes of the employees.

The chairman of the board or the chairman of the committee reviewing the administrative appointment should share with the principal the results of their evaluation. All information received from other sources should be handled in a professional and confidential way. Such an interview periodically is useful to the principal in setting his own improvement goals just as his interviews with those accountable to him are useful.

The principal may want to devise a form for obtaining teacher evaluation of his performance (see exhibit F). If he is brave enough, he may wish to summarize the results and share it with either the board chairman or the board itself.

EXHIBIT A

A PUPIL'S RATING SCALE OF A TEACHER

Teacher   Class   Date

Each of the qualities listed below is divided into three sections. Each section is divided into three degrees and numbered accordingly from one to nine, one being the highest degree and nine the lowest. In rating, draw a circle around the number which best describes your teacher.

Your fair and honest opinion is what really counts. Your teacher desires this rating for his own self-improvement.

Organization of the course	1 2 3	4 5 6	7 8 9
Teaching skill	1 2 3	4 5 6	7 8 9
Preparation for each class	1 2 3	4 5 6	7 8 9
Enthusiasm and interest	1 2 3	4 5 6	7 8 9
Assignments	1 2 3	4 5 6	7 8 9
Examinations	1 2 3	4 5 6	7 8 9
Class discussion and questions	1 2 3	4 5 6	7 8 9
Poise and self-confidence	1 2 3	4 5 6	7 8 9
Scholarship	1 2 3	4 5 6	7 8 9
Ability to create student interest	1 2 3	4 5 6	7 8 9
Class Management and discipline	1 2 3	4 5 6	7 8 9
Speech	1 2 3	4 5 6	7 8 9
Tolerance	1 2 3	4 5 6	7 8 9
Sense of humor	1 2 3	4 5 6	7 8 9
Personal appearance	1 2 3	4 5 6	7 8 9
Christian testimony	1 2 3	4 5 6	7 8 9
Teacher-student relationships	1 2 3	4 5 6	7 8 9

On the back of this form print any annoying mannerisms your teacher has developed which should be corrected. Also, print your criticisms of the course. This will be helpful to your teacher's self-improvement.

EXHIBIT B

TEACHER'S SELF-EVALUATION CHECKLIST

This checklist is concerned with the spiritual side of teaching and touches the reasons for which our Christian school exists. For a complete evaluation, this list should be supplemented with other available criteria which probe lesson preparation, teaching procedures, and professional attributes.

Name   Date

	Self-Rating			
	A	B	C	D
1. Do I pray for my students and colleagues consistently?	☐	☐	☐	☐
2. Do I have personal devotions consistently?	☐	☐	☐	☐
3. Am I engaged in Bible study?	☐	☐	☐	☐
4. Am I committing Scripture to memory?	☐	☐	☐	☐
5. Do I have a sensitivity for the lost?	☐	☐	☐	☐
6. Do I teach the needs of home and foreign missions?	☐	☐	☐	☐
7. Am I sensitive to the personal spiritual needs of my individual students?	☐	☐	☐	☐
8. Do I bring my students to specific points of decision?	☐	☐	☐	☐
9. Do I apply biblical principles in the development of attitudes, habits, values?	☐	☐	☐	☐
10. Do I apply biblical principles in discipline?	☐	☐	☐	☐
11. Do I integrate the Bible with my subject matter?	☐	☐	☐	☐
12. Do I teach tolerance and compassion for non-Christians and for Christians who hold differing views?	☐	☐	☐	☐
13. Do I encourage students to take an active part in their local churches?	☐	☐	☐	☐
14. Am I a faithful, active church member?	☐	☐	☐	☐
15. Do I encourage students to have an outreach through witnessing?	☐	☐	☐	☐
16. Are my relationships with my colleagues, students and parents sincere and open?	☐	☐	☐	☐

17. Do I have a feeling for the spiritual welfare of the school as a whole? ☐ ☐ ☐ ☐
18. Am I concerned about the spiritual level of the graduates and former students? ☐ ☐ ☐ ☐
19. Do I have a vision of Christian education which extends beyond my local school? ☐ ☐ ☐ ☐
20. Do I counsel with parents about the spiritual needs of their children? ☐ ☐ ☐ ☐
21. Does my life evoke enthusiasm among my students for the Christian life and service? ☐ ☐ ☐ ☐
22. Do I respect the authority of the administration of the school? ☐ ☐ ☐ ☐
23. Do I correct in myself the same attitudes and actions for which I correct my students? ☐ ☐ ☐ ☐

—Dr. Roy W. Lowrie, Jr. (Adapted)

EXHIBIT C

CONESTOGA VALLEY
SCHOOL DISTRICT

Teacher Observation—Conference

_____   _____   _____
Teacher's Name   Class Observed   Date

Nature of learning activity observed:

Commendations:

Recommendations:

Outcomes of Conference:

_____   _____
Teacher's Signature   Evaluator

EXHIBIT D

Class Analysis by Observation

Teacher Observed _____

Subject _____

Date and Period _____

I. **Classroom**
   A. Atmosphere ✓
      ____ Natural
      ____ Good
      ____ Stiff, rigid
      ____ Uncomfortable
      ____ Too warm
      ____ Too cold

   B. Appearance ✓
      ____ Very attractive
      ____ Neat and clean
      ____ Orderly in appearance
      ____ Average
      ____ Dirty

   C. Bulletin Boards (and other items on walls) ✓
      ____ Very attractive
      ____ Pleasant in appearance
      ____ Average
      ____ Poor
      ____ Need to be changed

   D. Bulletin Board Message
      ____ Easily understood
      ____ Understandable
      ____ Vague
      ____ No meaning

II. **Teacher**
   A. Appearance
      ____ Well groomed
      ____ Average
      ____ Needs improvement

B. Knowledge of Material (Preparation)
____ Well prepared
____ Adequately prepared
____ Shaky, needs improvement
____ Needs much more preparation

C. Presentation (Techniques)
____ Excellent
____ Good, interesting
____ Fair
____ Boring

D. Spiritual Application of Subject Matter
____ Apparent
____ Some
____ Little

III. Rapport with Pupils
____ Excellent
____ Good relationship
____ Teases too much
____ Picks favorites
____ Picks on some
____ Too aloof

IV. Discipline
____ Well established
____ Good
____ Average
____ Too strict
____ Too loose
____ Inconsistent

V. Personality
____ Pleasant
____ Moody
____ Grumpy

VI. Student Responsiveness
A. Knowledge attained (Subjective observation)
____ Excellent
____ Good
____ Average
____ Very little

B. Student Interaction with Teacher (Response)

___ Much

___ Some

___ Little

___ None

C. Student Behavior

___ On best behavior

___ Good behavior

___ Problems developing

___ Chaos

I have read this evaluation:_____

Teacher's Signature

_____   _____

Date   Principal's Signature

EXHIBIT E

Annual Teacher Evaluation Form

Code: S—Satisfactory; N—Needs Improvement

	S	**N**
I. Personal and Professional Qualities		
1. Evidences a meaningful relationship with Jesus Christ as Lord and Saviour.	___	___
2. Supports ideals of the school's sponsoring body.	___	___
3. Maintains a high standard of conduct and integrity.	___	___
4. Abides by school regulations.	___	___
5. Is prompt and accurate in fulfilling obligations.	___	___
6. Carries full share of extra-class responsibilities and enforcement of school standards.	___	___
7. Discusses school problems only with proper professional people.	___	___
8. Cooperative and open-minded to suggestions.	___	___
9. Makes use of opportunities for professional improvement.	___	___
10. Builds positive relationships with colleagues.	___	___

11. Respects worth, dignity, and individuality of each student.
12. Is emotionally controlled in trying circumstances.
13. Has a pleasant sense of humor.
14. Is forceful but not dogmatic in decision-making.
15. Is perceptive in evaluating own strengths and weaknesses.

II. Teaching Effectiveness

1. Does careful long-range and daily planning.
2. Has clear and specific objectives for teaching.
3. Individualizes assignments to needs of each student.
4. Uses enrichment and remedial materials to meet individual needs.
5. Provides opportunity for students to work independently on meaningful tasks.
6. Uses balanced variety of non-textual and non-print materials.
7. Involves students in planning and conducting class activities.
8. Is sensitive to student feelings and needs.
9. Has little need to use negative reinforcers to obtain positive behavior.
10. Provides a physically attractive environment for learning.
11. Is competent in academic knowledge of subject being taught.
12. Communicates knowledge effectively to students.
13. Emphasizes conceptual learning above rote learning.
14. Helps students apply learning to new situations.
15. Evaluates student work habits and attitudes.
16. Evaluates pupil progress on bases of class goals and individual ability.
17. Achieves a classroom atmosphere of enthusiasm for learning.

Written Statement of
Evaluation by the Principal

I have read this evaluation:_____
                            Teacher's Signature

_____   _____
Date   Principal's Signature

EXHIBIT F

ADMINISTRATION IMAGE QUESTIONNAIRE

Please respond to the following questions honestly and frankly in reference to your principal. Do not give your name; all responses are anonymous. Using the following code, circle the number which represents your reaction to each question:

1 = *Never*   3 = *Sometimes*   5 = *Always*
2 = *Seldom*   4 = *Usually*

WHAT IS YOUR OPINION
CONCERNING THE PRINCIPAL'S BEHAVIOR?

1. Does he express his ideas smoothly and articulately? 1 2 3 4 5
2. Is he patient, understanding, considerate, and courteous? 1 2 3 4 5
3. Does he show interest and enthusiasm toward his work? 1 2 3 4 5
4. Does he demonstrate a thorough knowledge and understanding of school administration? 1 2 3 4 5
5. Does he demonstrate the initiative and persistence needed to accomplish goals and objectives? 1 2 3 4 5
6. Does he support those responsible to him? 1 2 3 4 5
7. Does he adjust rapidly to changes in plans or procedures? 1 2 3 4 5
8. Does he function effectively under pressure? 1 2 3 4 5
9. Does he consider divergent views? 1 2 3 4 5
10. Does he encourage staff members to raise questions and express opinions? 1 2 3 4 5
11. Does he assign tasks to personnel capable of carrying them out? 1 2 3 4 5
12. Does he show a willingness to try new approaches or methods? 1 2 3 4 5
13. Does he clearly define and explain what is expected of staff members? 1 2 3 4 5
14. Does he treat staff members in an unbiased and impartial manner? 1 2 3 4 5
15. Does he create a feeling of unity and enthusiasm among those in contact with him? 1 2 3 4 5
16. Does he demonstrate a sense of humor at appropriate times? 1 2 3 4 5
17. Does he make effective decisions? 1 2 3 4 5

18. Does he effectively evaluate programs, practices, and personnel?   1 2 3 4 5
19. Does he coordinate the efforts of those responsible to him so that the organization operates at peak efficiency?   1 2 3 4 5
20. Is he conscious of the problems that exist on your level?   1 2 3 4 5
21. Does he maintain control of his emotions when things are not going right?   1 2 3 4 5
22. Does he demonstrate leadership which results in meeting important goals and objectives?   1 2 3 4 5
23. Are his grooming and attire appropriate?   1 2 3 4 5
24. Are his communications properly written and do they accurately express his thoughts and ideas?   1 2 3 4 5
25. Does he support the policies, procedures, and philosophy of the school board?   1 2 3 4 5
26. Does he create an atmosphere which is conducive to effectively meeting goals and objectives?   1 2 3 4 5
27. Does he create a sense of trustworthiness when interacting with him?   1 2 3 4 5
28. Is his Christian testimony clear and consistent?   1 2 3 4 5

If you wish, please list below one or more strengths of this administrator.

—Adapted from Kalamazoo (Mich.) Public Schools

"But select capable men from all the people—men who fear God, trustworthy men who hate dishonest gain—and appoint them as officials over thousands, hundreds, fifties and tens Have them serve as judges for the people at all times, but have them bring every difficult case to you; the simple cases they can decide themselves. That will make your load lighter, because they will share it with you" (Exod. 18:21-22).

"Do you see a man skilled in his work? He will serve before kings; he will not serve before obscure men" (Prov. 22:29).

"So Paul stayed for a year and a half, teaching them the word of God" (Acts 18:11).

"Do your best to present yourself to God as one approved, a workman who does not need to be ashamed and who correctly handles the word of truth" (2 Tim. 2:15).

"Wake up! Strengthen what remains and is about to die, for I have not found your deeds complete in the sight of my God" (Rev. 3:2).

8. In-service Development

In-service education denotes a planned program of professional growth for the personnel employed in a given school or system. It assumes a basic background of training for teaching. The purpose of in-service education is to build on that foundation to enable the employee to sharpen his skills and improve his performance in meeting the objectives of the school and of his specific job. The employing school need not provide the total in-service program by itself, but it should have policies that delineate the program and provide access to it.

An assumption behind an in-service program is that people can grow. Teachers are not "finished" professionals when they conclude their pre-service education; they need and can profit from an on-going professional development plan. A further assumption is that as teachers develop their competencies pupil learning will increase. That is of foundational importance inasmuch as schools exist to further the learning of those who are enrolled. In addition, new ideas in philosophy, content, and instruction come to the fore and are worthy of discussion.

Three characteristics of a good in-service program are that (1) it is planned, (2) the plan is implemented, and (3) the program is evaluated.

Planning the Program

To the extent that it is feasible, everyone involved in the program should be involved in the planning. A good way to get input from everyone is to poll the faculty annually regarding the needs they feel in their classrooms and in the school. An in-service planning committee or a committee to assist the principal in arranging faculty meetings helps employees to care about the program.

Such involvement of personnel helps the principal to determine the needs of the staff. Of course, as an educational leader he has his own observations and insights to give him clues to in-service needs. Nevertheless, the felt-needs of the staff are highly important.

Out of this input the school organizes an individualized inservice development program. It is individualized to the school and, as much as possible, it is tailored to the needs of each teacher.

Means of In-Service Development

Faculty meetings are no doubt the most common means of in-servicing a staff. There are three types of such meetings: (1) those that are for the discussion of school policies, goals, and procedures; (2) those that are for the stimulation of the teacher to professional excellence; and (3) those that encourage personal and group spiritual growth and commitment. All are necessary.

Frequently, teachers have negative feelings about faculty meetings. Such feelings can be ameliorated if meetings start and end on time, are not over-long (an hour maximum when held after school), are well planned (with teacher involvement), have pre-announced agendas, have relevant content, and clearly more toward a goal. If the faculty is large, they themselves will work at cross-purposes to these ideals. Many will want to speak (some at length and frequently); they will want to be involved in the decision-making, but they will find it difficult and perhaps impossible to arrive at consensus. Any principal will do well to pray for and seek to achieve the gift of chairing meetings with grace and efficiency.

Deciding the time for faculty meetings remains a difficult problem. Some schools experiment with before and after school sessions until they find the best time for their staff (sometimes a combination of times rather than always the same time). A good arrangement is to dismiss school an hour early and meet for a two-hour block. The writer knows of one school that begins school an hour late every Tuesday to achieve the same kind of arrangement. It is important that faculty meetings be scheduled and announced weeks and even months in advance so that teachers can plan their activities without time conflicts.

The meeting place should be arranged appropriately to the type of meeting: film, discussion, lecture, buzz groups, and so forth. A cup of coffee and a few cookies at times help to relax the teachers for good listening and sharing.

Many Christian schools have a daily prayer or devotional time every morning. The purpose of this activity should be clearly stated, attendance strongly encouraged if not required, and leadership rotated among the staff. In addition, spiritual understandings need to be integrated with and give guidance to professional understandings in all faculty meeting discussions. Occasional in-depth Bible studies can be helpful in faculty growth in spirituality and unity.

It is desirable to have one or more days before school opens in the fall for professional/spiritual stimulation and/or after school closes in the spring. A number of schools enjoy having these conferences as "retreats" in camp settings.

Supervision by the principal enables the employee to understand his task more clearly and to gain insight into how he might improve his performance. Demonstration teaching can be of help. Individual conferences are a necessity.

Supervision is helping teachers. The occasional person who may not seem to want help no doubt actually needs it the most. The one who would help must find out what is bothering the "turned-off" one. Perhaps he has feelings of insecurity in his personal and/or professional life. If so, he must be encouraged and commended at every opportunity for things he does well. Principals must offer help from an "along-side" stance rather than from an "I'm superior" position. The best help is that which helps teachers to help themselves.

Someone has suggested that the supervisory needs of teachers vary according to the following chart:

| new | — | orientation |
| older (in school) | — | recognition |

young	—	belonging
older (in years)	—	avoidance of change
inexperienced	—	skills
experienced	—	freedom
cooperative	—	avoidance of over-use
uncooperative	—	motivation
weak	—	security
strong	—	leadership
well	—	to be let alone
ill	—	diagnosis
substitute	—	knowledge

An important element of supervision for anyone is feedback. Everyone feels a need to know how he is doing—as perceived by his supervisor. This requires follow-up and continued communication after suggestions have been given and a plan of action devised.

Evaluations by various people—self, students, principal—encourage the discovery of strengths and weaknesses.

In his supervisory and evaluative role, the principal is in a position to individualize to each teacher an in-service program that meets his needs. A teacher may be asked to do a self-evaluation using questions such as these:

How do I help students achieve self-control?

What do I do to help make students enthusiastic about learning?

How do I evaluate pupil progress and growth?

How do I integrate Christian faith into my teaching?

What is my greatest strength and greatest weakness as a teacher?

How can I improve my teaching?

As teacher and principal share, a program of personalized professional improvement can emerge.

Memberships in professional organizations help keep teachers fresh and current in their teaching. **Participation** in these organizations encourages growth through the teachers' contributing to the professional development of others.

Subscriptions to professional magazines and purchase of relevant books stimulate professional improvement. School subscriptions to publications such as *The Master Teacher* for each faculty member are useful. Magazines and books placed in the faculty room or library are of limited value; too often such items are not picked up unless the teacher has immediate personal access when needed. Sometimes it is worthwhile to ask teachers to report their professional reading to the principal; occasionally an especially pertinent book can be the basis of faculty meeting discussion.

Teachers grow through individual experimentation in their classrooms. The school administration can set a wholesome atmosphere by encouraging guided experimenting with new techniques. "Status-quoism" never improved teaching or learning. Most teachers are afraid of failure in trying something new; they need strong support and counsel from the principal. That support includes his backing if the teacher receives criticism for what he is doing.

Curriculum development by the individual teacher, a committee, or the entire faculty provides valuable insights to teachers. Curriculum study will succeed only if strongly encouraged by the principal. He must allow it to begin with the "felt-needs" of the teachers regarding the instructional program.

School policy should encourage and financially support the continuing education of teachers. Not only should teachers seek advanced degrees, but they need refresher courses from time to time regardless of the degrees they may already possess. A recommended practice is for a school to require at least six graduate credits to be earned in each five-year period of employment.

Travel can be a means of professional growth. Obviously, it is highly relevant to the history teacher, but it can enrich the life of anyone. It is especially helpful if it takes one into other cultural settings. Persons who serve on foreign mission fields gain new perspectives for working with people of their own culture.

Participation in self-studies for a school's accreditation helps give teachers new understandings of their own school, its possibilities and its limitations. In fact, teacher growth is a chief value of the accreditation process even though it is a by-product of the effort.

Visiting the classrooms of other teachers is often a valuable growth experience. Such visits can be within the school or in another school. Occasionally, an in-service day can be used to have all the teachers out at the same time. Brief oral or written reports can help teachers think through the insights gained that can be applied to their own situations.

Evaluation of the In-Service Program

A key to an effective on-going program of in-service improvement is the evaluation of past programs. Did they meet teachers' needs? Why did they or did they not do so?

Evaluations can be conducted in various ways. They may take the form of a questionnaire following a faculty meeting, a conference with the principal after a teacher's experimentation with a new procedure, an oral or written report of a travel experience. It may be an annual survey of the year's in-service program to see what parts of it were most helpful.

A wise principal will use the evaluation results for program improvement. He will not do complete program flip-flops, however, just because of tallies in a survey. If some aspect of the in-servicing has a low rating, it may be that it needs to be developed differently rather than dropped completely. It is in the making of such decisions that a principal shows his leadership qualities and the worth of his salary.

A SUPERVISOR'S PRAYER[1]

by John Luther

Dear Lord, please help me—
To accept human beings as they are—not yearn for perfect creatures;
To recognize ability—and encourage it;
To understand shortcomings—and make allowance for them;
To work patiently for improvement—and not expect too much too quickly;
To appreciate what people do right—not just criticize what they do wrong;
To be slow to anger and hard to discourage;
To have the hide of an elephant and the patience of Job;
In short, Lord, please help me to be a better boss!

"The LORD would speak to Moses face to face, as a man speaks with his friend . . ." (Exod. 33:11).

"They read from the Book of the Law of God, making it clear and giving the meaning so that the people could understand what was being read" (Neh. 8:8).

"He who answers before listening—that is his folly and his shame" (Prov. 18:13).

"The purposes of a man's heart are deep waters, but a man of understanding draws them out" (Prov. 20:5).

"He who has ears, let him hear" (Matt. 11:15).

" 'No one ever spoke the way this man does,' the guards declared" (John 7:46).

"Then Jesus' disciples said, 'Now you are speaking clearly and without figures of speech' " (John 16:29).

"And pray for us, too, that God may open a door for our message, so that we may proclaim the mystery of Christ, for which I am in chains. Pray that I may proclaim it clearly, as I should" (Col. 4:3-4).

"We must pay more careful attention, therefore, to what we have heard, so that we do not drift away" (Heb. 2:1).

9. Communication

The principal of the school sets the tone for the quality of communication that occurs within the school. Of course, he is not the sole communicator, but if he is candid and an open person this will encourage openness on the part of others. If he is secretive, other members of the staff will tend to be that way and act independently rather than as a team.

Purposes of Communication

Castetter quotes from Thayer who identifies four functions of communication:
1. The informative function
2. Command and instruction function
3. Influence and persuasion function
4. Integrative function.[1]

Communication from the principal will be clearer and more effective if he defines the purpose of each communication effort. "Why am I telling the staff this?" There will be less ambiguity in the message and in the way it is heard, if he gives consideration to function before he writes or speaks.

Styles of Communication

Communication must have a two-way flow. It is necessary for the principal to be a good listener. He must sincerely seek to know and understand the opinions and the feelings of each staff member. He needs to treat what they say with respect, not gossiping to others about what they have shared with him. Yet, he also needs to be aware that those who are accountable to another tend to tell the manager what they suppose he wants to hear. "Reading between the lines," sensing nuances of meaning is a gift the principal needs in good measure. It is a hard lesson to learn that people do not always mean what they say. Communication is more, much more, than words.

Principal communication with staff should be primarily oral. Written communication tends to be more threatening and impersonal. In some situations a written follow-up to oral communication is desirable. For example, if a teacher is asked orally to serve as chairman of a study committee, that interchange should be followed by a memo that summarizes the understandings regarding the assignment that has been agreed upon. The written record helps the teacher to be clear on what the expectations are for him in the accepted assignment; it is all too easy to be unsure if a task is outlined orally only. One should not be upset when people forget the spoken instructions. Modern society is not geared to good listening. Recognizing that fact will help one to adjust his communication efforts appropriately.

General information can certainly be disseminated by written staff bulletins that are distributed weekly. In fact, this is much preferred to announcements that take up faculty meeting time. Notes of appreciation to individuals are also just as appropriate as the oral comment. Written reports of school board actions are desirable.

One of the points well made by Fred B. Chernow and Carol Chernow is that every teacher should be given "a copy of any publication before it is sent out to parents or pupils."[2] Teachers like to be informed in advance of anything that involves them. Just like everybody else, they dislike being surprised about something they feel a right to have known.

A good communicator will stop to talk with employees in their classrooms, shops, and cafeterias even though he has nothing to say. Just expressing interest tends to make employees feel important. They feel free to share their problems before they have become emotional mountains that cannot be leveled. The maintenance man in one school carried his gripes to board members he knew and threatened to resign because of having too much to do. He should not have handled his problem that way. One reason he did was that the principal had not made enough informal contacts with him. Therefore, the employee could not feel free to use proper channels of communication.

Use of Humor

Happy is that person who has cultivated the gift of humor so that he can delight as well as inform his listeners. Yet, it is easy to allow wit to degenerate into mere cleverness, and cleverness into the acid comment that hurts others by putting them down. Teachers and administrators, as persons in positions of power over others, need to ask the Lord for victory over this evil use of the tongue.

In one of his writings, Kenneth L. Pike shares a personal experience that teaches a valuable lesson:

When I was a freshman in college, I was part of a crew that served tables in the cafeteria, and a couple of the crew were the most accomplished fellows at barbed comments that I've ever met.

In competition with them I became clever, too, and by the end of that year I couldn't hear a sentence from one of my colleagues without thinking of something clever and sharp with which to reply.

When my Dad heard me, he would say, "Why don't people study to say the kind thing instead of the cruel thing?" But I couldn't think of anything encouraging, or sweet, or good. I had become totally corrupt. I could think only of the cruel thing, at which people had to laugh even if they were hurt.

I saw after a while that I was losing all my friends, and I asked God to break me of that habit. It took three years to break it, and in order to do so I had to swear before God that I'd be silent rather than say something barbed and cruel. I wasn't used to being silent and it hurt to have nothing to say when I was bursting with a clever remark. But God doesn't want us to look clever at the expense of someone else. We are called to serve, to make others look good.[3]

Communicating a Good Report

Claude E. Schindler, Jr., as superintendent of Dayton Christian Schools in Ohio, has committed himself and the school system he leads, to the practice of Matthew 18:15-17 in all matters of communication. He says, "Each of us must make a lifelong decision to give only a good report of others, unless we have followed the steps of Matthew 18 with a desire to restore the offender. This commitment of a good report should not only be made to the Lord, but also to every other member of our school family, to those with whom we have daily contact."[4] As a reminder to practice the biblical principles of good reports only about others unless they are first confronted, he has had printed reminders made available to all members of the school family:

GREAT

Good   Reports   Edify   and   Testify

Matthew 18:15-17

He sees the following outcomes when these principles are adhered to:
1. Gossip and slander will cease.
2. Loyalty within the organization will build security.
3. Christians will edify each other.
4. The world will believe.[5]

Handling Parent Complaints

Every principal at some time will receive a telephone call from an upset parent who is critical of teacher-treatment of his child. "Have you talked with the teacher about the matter?" is always a good response based on the principles of Matthew 18:15-17. If this approach by the parent has not succeeded from his viewpoint, the principal should arrange a conference between parents and teacher which he chairs. Before the meeting he should listen carefully to both sides of the case and get all the available and relevant facts. Few issues cannot be resolved in this way. Those that cannot, go to the board for final decision.

Teachers should know that they will be fully supported by the administration so long as they have adhered to school policies. Even when they did not, their reprimanding should be in private. Parents, too, should have the confidence that their concerns will be carefully listened to and respected.

Communicating to the Public

Communication for good personnel relations goes beyond the staff itself. It includes informing the entire school community of the achievements of the school and members of the staff. When a teacher earns an advanced degree, attends or directs a professional workshop, or achieves other recognition, the principal should inform the student body, the board, the parents, and the general school public of this. In addition to using school releases, newspapers will send their reporters to cover events of special significance.

Although such publicity falls within the general job description of the principal, he may want to delegate the task to a staff member or volunteer who enjoys writing news releases.

"Now the Ephraimites asked Gideon, 'Why have you treated us like this? Why didn't you call us when you went to fight Midian?' And they criticized him sharply.

"But he answered them, 'What have I accomplished compared to you? Aren't the gleanings of Ephraim's grapes better than the full grape harvest of Abiezer? God gave Oreb and Zeeb, the Midianite leaders, into your hands. What was I able to do compared to you?' At this, their resentment against him subsided" (Judges 8:1-3).

"The words of a gossip are like choice morsels; they go down to a man's inmost parts.

"An offended brother is more unyielding than a fortified city, and disputes are like the barred gates of a citadel" (Prov. 18:8, 19).

"Without wood a fire goes out; without gossip a quarrel dies down. As charcoal to embers and as wood to fire, so is a quarrelsome man for kindling strife" (Prov. 26:20-21).

"They dress the wound of my people as though it were not serious. 'Peace, peace,' they say, when there is no peace" (Jer. 8:11).

"Do everything in love" (1 Cor. 16:14).

"Bear with each other and forgive whatever grievances you may have against one another. Forgive as the Lord forgave you. And over all these virtues put on love, which binds them all together in perfect unity" (Col. 3:13-14).

"Make every effort to live in peace with all men and to be holy; without holiness no one will see the Lord. See to it that no one misses the grace of God and that no bitter root grows up to cause trouble and defile many" (Heb. 12:14-15).

10. Grievance Procedures

Whenever people need to work together in close relationships there are possibilities for misunderstandings among them. These misunderstandings generally arise out of a difference of perspective that makes it easy to look at a matter from one point of view but not from any other. These differences are brought on by varied backgrounds of experiences. To a larger extent than most of us care to admit, we are prisoners of our past experiences.

Christians often find it difficult to admit that there can be misunderstandings among brothers and sisters. Such a position does not do away with disagreements; it only shoves them "under the carpet" where all who face reality see the "bulge of stumbling" though they may not know specifically what is there.

As American Christians we have much to learn regarding openness and avoiding the defensiveness that normally accompanies a person in a power position, such as in Christian school administration. Walking in humility before God and one's fellowmen and establishing procedures for handling grievances will make for a happier staff and will honor the name of Christ.

Definition of Grievance

A grievance is a complaint by an employee suggesting that he has been treated unfairly according to the policies/procedures of the organization. The unfair treatment may be real or imagined, but it must be understood that it is real to the complainant. Whether real or not, it is important to good morale that the employee know how to handle his gripe without fear of reprisal and without resorting to gossip and slanderous accusations. The latter is sin, but the employee may yield to the temptation of sin because of a principal whom he sees as unapproachable and arrogant, or because he is frustrated by lack of policies to give him guidance. The sin of a principal or board never justifies a sinful response from an employee, but neither dare a leader hide his wrongdoing behind that of an employee.

Principles for Handling Grievances

In Matthew 18:15-17 the Lord Jesus gives a timeless and classic statement on the handling of sins in the community of faith. The principles apply to grievances in employer-employee relationships and are found useful by management counselors in all situations, Christian or otherwise.

> If your brother sins against you, go and show him his fault, just between the two of you. If he listens to you, you have won your brother over. But if he will not listen, take one or two others along, so that "every matter may be established by the testimony of two or three witnesses." If he refuses to listen to them, tell it to the church; and if he refuses to listen even to the church, treat him as you would a pagan or a tax collector.

Principle No. 1—The complaint should be settled at the lowest level of relationship possible.

Therefore, the aggrieved employee comes directly to the principal and states his complaint orally. If the principal recognizes the complaint as justified and that the employee has been "sinned against," he takes whatever steps are necessary to rectify the wrong. He may be able to handle it directly by saying: "I was wrong; I'll correct the matter today." He may need to say: "You seem to have a just complaint. Let me check with the bookkeeper to see if we can clarify the situation and correct it if there is an error. I'll get back to you before the end of the week." He may need to say, "I see your point. I don't know what the board had in mind, but I'll check it out with the chairman. He may want to bring it to the next meeting for clarification. I'll keep you informed."

Many minor complaints that could turn into major grievances are handled in this way and solved promptly. That is beautiful when it can be done so simply and graciously. But it does not always work out that way.

Principle No. 2—If the complaint cannot be settled between principal and employee, the employee should go to the next higher authority until he gets relief or a final "no" from the last authority.

In most Christian schools, the chief administrative officer is the principal. If, however, there is an officer over him, for example, a superintendent, the employee should carry his grievance to the superintendent if he is dissatisfied with the response he received from the principal. After the superintendent, the court of last appeal is the board. If the board refuses any redress, the employee must accept their decision gracefully. If he cannot do so, he has no alternative but to resign for otherwise "a root of bitterness" will spring up in his heart to destroy the effectiveness of his own Christian witness and that of the school as a unity.

It is important that at each level of "hearing" the grievance, the person or persons charged with decision making seek to be as open to truth as possible. They should not merely support an administrative officer as a matter of course. He could be in error, and, if so, that error must be acknowledged and corrected. In order to make wise judgments, all facts that impinge on the case need to be assembled from every available source.

Chernow and Chernow give six tips for handling complaints:

1. Listen with interest.
2. Dignify the complaint.
3. Remain poised.
4. Assemble the facts.
5. Be direct.
6. Stick with the decision.[1]

They assert that denying an employee's request requires excellent human relations skills. Saying no is never easy for a person who has a high regard for his colleagues. Honest, clearcut, and understandable reasons should be given for the negative decision. "Reasons that are clear and understandable from the teacher's point of view should always be a part of rendering a negative decision."[2] One might add that there will be times when the reasons do not make sense to the emotionally involved employee, but the principal should seek to be as open and candid as he can. Nothing can help as much as a genuine feeling of empathy even though one disagrees with his position.

Need for Board Policies

Policy statements regarding grievances should be adopted by every school board. Such statements should include definitions, the procedures for redress, and the guarantee of protection for the employee who follows procedures. Employees should have full knowledge of these policies and procedures through the pages of the faculty handbook (see exhibit A).

With the adoption of clear policies by the school board, there is no excuse for employees to gossip their complaints to fellow employees, friends, or even to board members before the case reaches board level of decision making. Any employee who expresses disloyalty in this way either thoughtlessly or maliciously must be confronted in Christian love by the principal. In this reversal of roles, the principles of Matthew 18 apply equally as with the aggrieved employee.

Trust, goodwill, and openness must characterize employer-employee relationships in the Christian school. If they do not, it is incumbent upon the board to determine the causes of suspicion, secrecy, and ill will, and to remove those causes. Antagonisms in personnel relationships will destroy the work of God in the school.

EXHIBIT A

PROFESSIONAL EMPLOYEE TENURE POLICIES

1. If circumstances should necessitate a decrease in number of professional employees, seniority shall be given high priority in determining who shall be retained on the staff.

2. The administration of the Lancaster Mennonite High School and the Board of Trustees covenant that in any case of board-initiated termination or non-renewal of contract, they shall in the spirit of brotherhood individually and collectively seek to help the faculty member find employment that fits his gifts.

3. No professional employee shall have his services terminated due to an unsatisfactory administrative evaluation unless there is evidence that there was a continuing effort on the part of the administration to communicate with the employee regarding unsatisfactory aspects of his service that were considered.

4. Appeal Procedures for Professional Employees:

   a. In case an impasse develops between the administrator and the professional employee regarding the latter's having his contract terminated or not renewed, the professional employee may appeal his case to the Personnel Committee of the Board of Trustees.

   b. The Personnel Committee shall arrange separate and private interviews with the professional employee, the appropriate instructional leader (if any), the administrator, and any other persons the Committee believes have insight regarding the matter in order that they may obtain as balanced perspective as possible.

   c. The Personnel Committee shall report their findings with recommendations to the Board of Trustees.

   d. If the action of the Board of Trustees is not acceptable to the professional employee, he may appeal through the Personnel Committee for a personal hearing before the entire Board of Trustees.

   e. Following the personal hearing, the Board of Trustees shall take final action that shall close the case.

   f. All voting for termination or non-renewal of contracts shall require a 75 percent majority of board members present.

"*That night the king could not sleep; so he ordered the book of the chronicles, the record of his reign, to be brought in and read to him. It was found recorded there that Mordecai had exposed Bigthana and Teresh, two of the king's officers, who guarded the doorway and who had conspired to assassinate King Xerxes. 'What honor and recognition has Mordecai received for this?' the king asked. 'Nothing has been done for him,' his attendants answered*" (Esther 6:1-3).

"*So I bought the field at Anathoth from my cousin Hanamel and weighed out for him seventeen shekels of silver. I signed and sealed the deed, had it witnessed, and weighed out the silver on the scales. I took the deed of purchase—the sealed copy containing the terms and conditions, as well as the unsealed copy—and I gave this deed to Baruch son of Neriah, the son of Mahseiah, in the presence of my cousin Hanamel and of the witnesses who had signed the deed and of all the Jews sitting in the courtyard of the guard. In their presence I gave Baruch these instructions: 'This is what the LORD Almighty, the God of Israel, says: Take these documents, both the sealed and the unsealed copies of the deed of purchase, and put them in a clay jar so they will last a long time. For this is what the LORD Almighty, the God of Israel, says: Houses, fields and vineyards will again be bought in this land'*" (Jer. 32:9-15).

"*Many have undertaken to draw up an account of the things that have been fulfilled among us, just as they were handed down to us by those who from the first were eyewitnesses and servants of the word. Therefore, since I myself have carefully investigated everything from the beginning, it seemed good also to me to write an orderly account for you, most excellent Theophilus, so that you may know the certainty of the things you have been taught*" (Luke 1:1-4).

11. Office Records

A comprehensive set of personnel records serves several useful functions: (1) It provides the factual information that is routinely needed in school administration. Examples are the number of sick days a teacher has accumulated, his classification by virtue of experience and training for salary determination, expiration date of teaching certificate. (2) It provides the data base for analysis of trends and personnel problems. (3) It enables the principal to give efficient and wise counsel to individual teachers.

Personnel Folders

An individual file should be kept on each employee. Many schools use plain manila folders into which pertinent memos, letters, forms, and so forth, are placed. Others use folders that are published for this purpose with various types of data charts printed on both sides of the folder. Some larger schools choose to have their own folders printed to accommodate the particular kind of data needed. The printed folders are preferable because they avoid the clutter of many pieces of paper in folders that quickly become too thick.

Personnel folders should be kept current. Material should be added as soon as available; useless material should be weeded annually. In fact, each folder should be reviewed every summer to assure that items are up to date and correct.

These files should be housed in the principal's office. This placement gives him ready access to them and helps maintain their confidentiality. If they are located in a secretary's office, there is less guarantee that they will be secure from unauthorized persons.

Information to Be Filed

Examples of information to include in each personnel folder are the following:

1. Application for employment
2. Copies of signed contracts
3. Reports of physical examinations
4. Record of absences
5. Record of accumulated sick-leave days
6. Record of employment
7. Reports on classroom observations
8. Annual evaluation reports
9. Transcripts of all college credits
10. Copies of teaching certificates
11. Intention to return forms
12. Personal and family information
13. Awards and recognitions
14. Exchange of personal memos
15. Copies of correspondence with or about employee

Copies of withholding tax forms (W-4s) and similar forms may be in the personnel file but will more likely be housed in the office of the bookkeeper, business manager, or treasurer.

Every office needs a rubber date stamp. As each piece of information is received, it should be dated before being placed in the file. Dating papers when received helps answer questions that may arise in the future.

Collective Personnel Information

In addition to a folder for each employee, the principal should have a folder(s) where he keeps current accumulated data on all employees. A chart showing years of employment for all personnel consolidates into one handy reference individual and group information. If physical examinations are required on a regular basis, this information can be charted for ease in reminding those whose exams are coming due. Certification expirations, absences (sick and personal), salary levels are some of the kinds of data that could be useful on a composite graph or table.

"He has filled them with skill to do all kinds of work as craftsmen, designers, embroiderers in blue, purple and scarlet yarn and fine linen, and weavers—all of them master craftsmen and designers" (Exod. 35:35).

"Who will listen to what you say? The share of the man who stayed with the supplies is to be the same as that of him who went down to the battle. All will share alike" (1 Sam. 30:24).

"Now that I, your Lord and Teacher, have washed your feet, you also should wash one another's feet" (John 13:14).

"The man who plants and the man who waters have one purpose, and each will be rewarded according to his own labor" (1 Cor. 3:8).

"Yes, and I ask you, loyal yokefellow, help these women who have contended at my side in the cause of the gospel, along with Clement and the rest of my fellow workers, whose names are in the book of life" (Phil. 4:3).

12. Support Staff

Most employees in the Christian school are persons with professional preparation and competence. However, these teachers and administrators cannot perform their work most effectively without the support of others: secretaries, maintenance-custodial personnel, and, in some schools, cafeteria workers. In addition, every school needs a corps of professional part-time persons, the substitute teachers who become classroom leaders when regular teachers are absent. The care of these employees needs the special touch of the principal lest they be neglected and feel unappreciated for their work, often performed more or less behind the scenes.

Substitute Teachers

With some modifications the qualifications for substitute teachers should be similar to the qualifications of the personnel in whose places they serve. They are employed to replace the absentee with as little learning loss to the students as possible. Therefore, they need special abilities in understanding children, strong leadership attributes, and flexibility. Because they will be called upon to substitute in a variety of classrooms, their preparation in a specific academic field counts for less than with the regular teacher.

Substituting is one of the most difficult and thankless jobs in a school. Because the substitute cannot build rapport with students during a long-term continuing relationship, the way he "sells" himself each day is crucial.

One can recruit substitutes in the community from among pastors, retired teachers, and former teachers now become homemakers. They should go through the same selection processes as regular staff. A new substitute needs orientation to the school and to his work. It might be provided in the regular new-teacher orientation before school opens or at a special session with the principal. A substitute needs continuing orientation because he misses learning about many of the changes in procedures that are known to the full-time staff.

Communication, therefore, becomes especially important to the substitute. He should have a mailbox in the school with other staff persons and receive the same information pieces they receive. Including substitutes in school social events helps give them a sense of belonging and of involvement.

In order for the substitute to serve most effectively, the principal needs to assure that the regular teacher will make the transition as easy as possible. Helps in doing this are the preparation of the students for the substitute, provision of a current seating chart and lesson plans with specific directions and suggested time allotments, and cooperative planning by telephone if possible.

On the other hand, the regular teacher has a right to expect that the substitute will follow his written plans as closely as possible, leave materials provided and pupil work collected at an agreed-upon place, and write a note summarizing what went on during the day.

The board needs to review annually the compensation schedule for substitutes. Normally they are paid on a per diem basis at a rate that is somewhat below that of a full-time professional. This per diem wage can appropriately be the total financial compensation rather than to include the welfare and other fringe benefits of regular employees. If the substitute is needed on a quasi-full-time basis, there would be justification for reviewing the compensation arrangement toward more equal treatment with those employed full time. Generally being small, most Christian schools need only occasional substitutes.

Non-faculty

Non-faculty, too, need loving care from their principal and the professional colleagues. A cook is seldom noticed unless the salt is forgotten in the peas; a custodian, unless a classroom is dirty; a maintenance person, unless the water fountain does not work. Secretaries receive more attention, but sometimes it is an upset parent, an over-tired teacher, or an angry student who gives the attention. All of these people tend to be nameless servants to the school's public. When prayers are made for staff or appreciations are expressed, they are usually—thoughtlessly, of course—for "teachers and administrators." It is often somewhat difficult for these support people to feel that they are involved in Christian service the same as are the teachers. Therefore, the principal and the board need to use their leadership positions to underscore the value of support persons to the total professional staff.

Yearbook dedications, participation in graduation processions, invitations to give chapel talks, friendly "hello's" and inquiries about their work, social fellowship with the faculty—these are a few of the ways to say to them that they are important members of the school team.

Recruitment and selection of non-faculty employees is as important as for the professional, but it is carried out in somewhat different settings (see exhibits A, B, and C for application forms). One begins with a well-developed job description so he can articulate exactly what kind of person he is seeking. He will advertise his needs wherever persons with the desired qualifications may likely be found. Newsletters to parents, bulletin announcements in supporting churches, and ads in local, denominational, or broad circulation periodicals can be helpful. For secretaries, an additional source is Christian high schools and colleges with career business programs.

School boards are sometimes inclined to feel that the spiritual qualifications of non-faculty are of less importance than of teachers. Such a position can lower the school's spiritual temperature and decrease the freedom and power of the Holy Spirit to work. Every employee contributes to the school's atmosphere in a positive or negative way. A quarrelsome or discontented custodian can badly infect the school. Compensation of non-faculty employees takes careful study and wise policy making. Should they be compensated on the same levels as professional employees? Should they receive more because they have less prestige? Should they be paid less because they work on an hourly basis? In many Christian schools non-faculty persons are paid at more nearly the secular wage scale than are teachers. It seems necessary to do this because so few people feel the call to this type of service. Because fringe benefits have generally been added for professionals to stretch their compensation dollars and because their salaries are low by secular school standards, should relatively higher-paid non-faculty people receive the same benefits as the teachers (see exhibit D)?

Whatever specific answers to these questions are determined, compensation policy should adhere to the principles of need, Christian brotherhood, and justice. Although regular living requirements may be similar for all employees, the requirements of extended professional training for teachers has salary and benefits implications. Experience is a factor that merits salary recognition regardless of the type work that is done.

Non-faculty employees should be given job orientation and in-service training experiences. The latter are available at seminars for secretaries and for maintenance-custodial personnel. If none can be found through local organizations, one can try planning some workshops in cooperation with other Christian organizations in the area.

Supervision and evaluation of work performance are as important for support personnel as for teachers. In small schools the principal will generally carry responsibility for these tasks; in larger schools they may be delegated to the business manager or another administrator.

Volunteers

For reasons of economy and parent involvement, some Christian schools use unpaid volunteers as support staff, especially for custodial work. The principles of good human relations apply in such circumstances also, perhaps more so, because volunteers often do not feel as deep a commitment to the school as do paid employees. Orientation sessions, clear instructions, supervision, and words of appreciation are necessary components of a strong volunteer program.

EXHIBIT A

NORFOLK CHRISTIAN SCHOOLS

Application for Staff Employment (Non-teaching)

Position applying for _____ Date of Application _____

Would you work full time? (hours compatible with school session) _____

or part time? _____ Specify approximate amount of time _____

Would you be able to work during the summer?

Full time _____ Part time _____ or not at all _____ .

Give earliest possible date you would be available to begin work_____

Comments _____

PERSONAL INFORMATION (Please enclose a picture if possible) _____

Name _____ Social Security No. _____
      Last   First   Middle Initial

Address _____ Telephone No. _____
         No. Street   City   State   Zip

Date of Birth _____ Marital Status: Single ☐ Married ☐ Other _____

Name of Spouse _____

Names and ages of children_____

Physical Disabilities (Describe any serious illness in health background):

Church now attending _____

Testimony to salvation and personal relationship with Christ _____

Why do you desire to work at NCS? _____

Do you understand and agree with the Statement of Faith and Purpose of NCS's ministry? _____

Do you use tobacco or liquor?_____

EDUCATION AND TRAINING

Circle last year completed	Name of school/college	Diploma or Degree earned
High School 1 2 3 4		
College 1 2 3 4		

Other training such as Business School, Technical, etc.

WORK EXPERIENCE

Employer	Address	Position Held	From/To	Reason for Leaving

OTHER EXPERIENCE: (Please list any additional experience you have had which would be useful in the ministry of NCS such as teaching Sunday School or working in any way with children; driving; office work; skills)

REFERENCES (Give names and addresses)

1. A spiritual leader_____

2. A person who has known you for many years (not a relative)_____

_____

3. A work supervisor _____

EXHIBIT B

DAYTON CHRISTIAN SCHOOLS, INC.
325 Homewood Avenue
Dayton, Ohio 45405   513/278-9645

CLERICAL EMPLOYMENT REFERRAL FORM

Name of applicant _____ Date_____

Position applied for_____ Your Phone No. _____

What characteristics and qualities does this person manifest and exhibit which show spiritual growth?

Please describe the applicant's:	Excellent	Good	Fair	Poor
a) willingness to learn	☐	☐	☐	☐
b) acceptance of authority	☐	☐	☐	☐
c) initiative	☐	☐	☐	☐
d) leadership	☐	☐	☐	☐
e) friendliness	☐	☐	☐	☐
f) cooperativeness	☐	☐	☐	☐
g) ability to accept responsibility	☐	☐	☐	☐
h) ability to keep confidences	☐	☐	☐	☐
i) general daily attitude	☐	☐	☐	☐
j) appearance	☐	☐	☐	☐

Please describe the applicant's abilities at:

	Excellent	Good	Fair	Poor
a) typing (speed/accuracy)	☐	☐	☐	☐
b) shorthand	☐	☐	☐	☐
c) office machines	☐	☐	☐	☐
d) telephone manners	☐	☐	☐	☐
e) filing	☐	☐	☐	☐
f) handling people	☐	☐	☐	☐
g) bookkeeping	☐	☐	☐	☐

How long have you known the applicant?

What are the specific qualities this person manifested which would cause you to desire to retain him/her?

What position did he/she hold for you?

Signed _____ Position_____

—Please use reverse side for any additional pertinent comments—

EXHIBIT C

LANCASTER MENNONITE HIGH SCHOOL
2176 Lincoln Highway East
Lancaster, PA 17602

APPLICATION FOR EMPLOYMENT

Mr.
Mrs.
Miss _____ Date of application _____

Last Name   First   Middle

Area

Address _____ Telephone _____ Code _____

_____ Social Security No. _____
Zip Code

Date of Birth _____ Are you a citizen of the United States? _____
Month Day Year

Physical handicaps and condition of health during last two years _____

Marital status: Single ☐ Married ☐ Widowed ☐ Divorced ☐ Separated ☐

Number of children _____ Their ages _____

Church membership _____

Position applying for: _____

Qualifications for position applied for: Degree-

Education: Name of institution   Location Subject   Dates attended   year ____
High school _____   _____ _____   19__ to 19__   _____
College _____   _____ _____   19__ to 19__   _____
Other _____   _____ _____   19__ to 19__   _____

Experience: Employer   Type of work   Years ____
_____   _____   19__ to 19__
_____   _____   19__ to 19__
_____   _____   19__ to 19__

Other:
_____   _____   19__ to 19__
_____   _____   19__ to 19__
_____   _____   19__ to 19__

What hours and days of week would you be available? _____

Character References:

_____   _____
Name of employer   Address and phone number

_____   _____
Name of pastor   Address and phone number

_____   _____
Name of friend (no relative)   Address and phone number

Minimum wage rate that would be acceptable to you? _____

Enclose a statement identifying the kinds of qualities and skills that you would be bringing to the job that would qualify you for the position. Also give the one area that you feel least qualified for in this position.

Statement of Faith:
A) Write a brief statement including your personal relationship to Christ, your present relationship to the church and how these relationships influence your everyday life and commitment.
B) Are you willing to be guided by the sponsoring board of trustees, the Lancaster Mennonite Conference, and the administration of the school? Are you open to consider changes in life and conduct that may be requested by these groups?
C) Comments or questions?

EXHIBIT D

DAYTON CHRISTIAN SCHOOLS, INC.

SECRETARIAL/CLERICAL SALARY SCHEDULE

QUALIFICATIONS:
1. Born-Again Believer
2. Experience in area of employment
3. References
4. Regular church attendance and active participation
5. Education–high school minimum

Effective date:
August 1, 1979

Contract year:
August 1 to July 31

EXPERIENCE*		SALARY** (H.S. to 2 yrs. college)	SALARY (2+ yrs. college)	Hourly Rate
Y	0	$6,032.00	$6,182.00	$2.90
E	1	6,136.00	6,286.00	2.95
A	2	6,240.00	6,390.00	3.00
R	3	6,344.00	6,494.00	3.05
S	4	6,448.00	6,598.00	3.10
	5	6,552.00	6,702.00	3.15
E	6	6,656.00	6,806.00	3.20
X	7	6,760.00	6,910.00	3.25
P	8	6,864.00	7,014.00	3.30
E	9	6,968.00	7,118.00	3.35
R	10	7,072.00	7,222.00	3.40
I	11	7,176.00	7,326.00	
E	12	7,280.00	7,430.00	
N	13	7,384.00	7,534.00	
C	14	7,488.00	7,638.00	
E	15	7,592.00	7,742.00	

*Experience in Christian schools counts full, while experience in a similar secular job will be credited at 50% of D.C.S. scale, not exceeding ten (10) years.
**All salary figures are based on 52 weeks per year/40 hours per week.

Vacation Policy:
Paid vacations are earned after the following years of seivice at D.C.S.:

(a) 1-2 years . . . . 1 week   *Only employees working 30 hours or*
(b) 2-5 years . . . . 2 weeks   *more per week for a minimum of 12*
(c) 6 years and up . . . . . . 3 weeks   *months of the year are eligible for*
                                              vacation pay.
Vacation pay is based on the average number of weekly hours worked over the course of a year.

Holidays:
The following are paid holidays for full-time employees:

Presidents' Day . . . . 1 day	Labor Day . . . . 1 day
Easter (Good Friday) . . . . . 1 day	Thanksgiving . . . . 2 days
Memorial Day . . . . 1 day	Christmas . . . . 2 days
July 4 . . . . 1 day	New Year's . . . . 2 days

Sick Leave—Paid:
Five (5) days per year (accumulate to 20 days)

Personal Days—Paid:
One (1) day per year (not accumulated)

Emergency Days—Paid:
Two (2) days per year (not accumulated)

Tuition Reductions: (Based on years of experience at D.C.S.)
0-5 years: 1st child—10%; 2nd child—30%; third child—50%; 4th child—70%
5 yrs and over: 1st child—25%; 2nd child—45%; third child—65%; 4th child—85%

Insurance:
Option to join Group Medical Plan. Single contracts paid.
Disability and Life Insurance provided for each full-time employee.

Hours:
Secretarial:
During school operation: 7:30 a.m. to 4:00 p.m. (1/2 hour for lunch)
During summer: 8:00 a.m. to 4:00 p.m. (1/2 hour for lunch)

Extra Hours:
Being requested to work on Saturdays by an administrator constitutes extra hours
Rate: First 8 hours or part of that . . . . $4.00 per hour
Anything beyond 8 hours . . . . $4.75 per hour

"He has showed you, O man, what is good. And what does the LORD require of you? To act justly and to love mercy and to walk humbly with your God" (Micah 6:8).

"If a house is divided against itself, that house cannot stand" (Mark 3:25).

"When I was a child, I talked like a child, I thought like a child, I reasoned like a child. When I became a man, I put childish ways behind me" (1 Cor. 13:11).

"Do everything without complaining or arguing" (Phil. 2:14).

". . . give thanks in all circumstances, for this is God's will for you in Christ Jesus" (1 Thess. 5:18).

"And let us consider how we may spur one another on toward love and good deeds" (Heb. 10:24).

13. Morale

The morale of a group of employees is the sum total of their feelings about themselves individually, themselves as a group, their work, their work incentives, and their managers. As a complex and sometimes vague entity, morale is constantly moving on a continuum between high and low.

High morale is evidenced by happy employees who work together as a team toward their common goal. Low morale is characterized by disgruntled employees with strongly independent actions, high rates of absenteeism, and lack of loyalty to the organization.

The whole personnel effort of a Christian school principal is to build and maintain a high level of morale among all employees. He and the school board largely set the level of morale by their attitudes and the policies they establish. There is a very real sense in which this entire book has been dealing with factors that determine staff morale; this chapter is a kind of summary on the subject.

Causes of Low Morale

One might assume that employees in a Christian school would all be high-morale persons. They joined the staff because they believed God led them to do so. They came out of deep service-to-Christ motivation rather than just to get a job. They practice prayer and daily commitment of their lives to God. They seek the guidance of the Holy Spirit in their work.

Sometimes such persons join the Christian school staff with joy and excitement that is contagious. Gradually and subtly a change occurs. They find that the saints on earth among whom they move are sometimes hard to love. They find themselves drained emotionally, physically, and spiritually from overwork. The students are unresponsive; the parents disinterested. When this change occurs, perhaps it is because their orientation to the school was not geared to reality, or they were not led on toward personal, spiritual, and professional maturity.

Sometimes a point can be made effectively by stating goals in a negative manner. David E. Lee does this by offering ways that are guaranteed to produce alienation within the school:

Keep your teachers in the dark and feed them erroneous information. Establish a feeling among your teachers that something is going on that they do not know about. Even the least important information sometimes can be considered very important by the teachers.

Show partiality to a few of your teachers and neglect the others. Spend all your time talking and consulting with these "privileged" few. Always appoint them as committee members, brag about them in front of the other teachers, and anytime you need help, go to them.

Keep teachers' salaries as low as possible, but expect a million dollars' worth of work from them. Provide no incentive pay for those conscientious teachers who go back to school to better themselves professionally. Provide only a slight increase in pay for teachers with a master's degree.

Give your teachers rigid schedules to meet at the last minute. Even though you have had all year to plan for this, put them under stress and make them work diligently until the work is complete.

Create jobs in your district for those individuals who have exhibited incompetence in their previous positions. They will have the respect and cooperation of every teacher on the staff.

Do not attempt to provide safeguards against the belligerent behavior of some students. Let the teachers know they are stuck with these misbehaving students. Always side with the student when disciplinary problems arise.

Cater to teachers who complain the most about conditions in the school. Pacify them to keep them satisfied. The other teachers really don't mind.

Do not attempt to provide financial aid for teacher materials. A good teacher doesn't need anything except a classroom full of students. Supplementary material isn't needed for the slower or faster student, because good teachers possess magic in their teaching styles. Never make yourself available to the teachers. After all, teachers shouldn't need any assistance if they are doing their jobs. When the teachers talk to you always be in a hurry, have all the answers for them, and, most of all, make them feel that you are too busy to talk to them.

Take all the credit when your school is recognized for its achievement and blame the teachers when your school is criticized.[1]

Bases for High Morale

By attention to certain key issues, the principal can do much to keep a high level of staff morale. Greene points out that good morale tends to be associated with:

1. Receiving recognition for doing a job well.
2. Having opportunities for participation in decision making.
3. Being able to provide a service or a skill which is appreciated by others.
4. Enjoying the job one has to perform.
5. Appreciating the leadership under which one works.
6. Feeling secure in knowing where one stands with his peers.
7. Being able to predict or to understand administrative decisions rather than being surprised by them or resentful of them.
8. Experiencing straightforwardness and friendliness from administrators.[2]

He states further: "Morale is not a single characteristic. High salaries alone cannot buy good morale nor can extensive fringe benefits. Good morale is more subtly related to the inner needs of man, his ego, his need and desire to be a participating part of a group, his drive to be something unique."[3]

Helping Staff Feel Good About Themselves

Believing that it is true that good morale is a factor of how a person feels about himself in the totality of his job situation, the principal sets himself to building self-concepts. The first way he does this is by exhibiting his own positive self-image. Leaders who like themselves and enjoy their own companionship serve as models for others. It is not wrong to like oneself although some Christians have unfortunately labeled a feeling of self-worth "pride." Small wonder some neighbors have felt so little love: "Love your neighbor as yourself" (Matt. 22:39).

The second way the principal builds the self-concept of his employees is by genuinely liking them. He makes them feel accepted, wanted, competent, and appreciated. Each of them can say, "I like me," because he perceives that "others (including the principal) like me." What a beautiful picture this is of what God has done for us: He accepted us so that we can accept ourselves!

Liking the employees means the principal feels good about them. He felt good about them when he hired them for they were God's gifts to the school in answer to prayer and searching. He continues to feel good about them as he helps them understand their tasks and the school goals. He communicates expectations and how to reach them. He helps them to evaluate realistically how well they are succeeding.

"He likes them" does not mean he is fawning over them or is gushy with praise. He may send birthday cards, or even take them out to lunch on birthdays; he may give a red rose on a wedding anniversary. He may pray with them or send notes of appreciation for jobs well done. The "how" he expresses love is less important than that it is expressed—genuinely, naturally, sincerely.

Morale-Boosting Principals

In a study of five administrators who were successfully meeting the challenge of working with people, Dale Richard Wynn found fourteen descriptors that are useful as measuring sticks for all who would be strong personnel administrators:

1. They find a lively and enduring interest and enjoyment in working with people.
2. They have an abiding faith and confidence in people.

3. They establish warm and friendly rapport with people quite easily.
4. They treat individuals equally and fairly.
5. They possess a keen sensitivity to the feelings and reactions of people.
6. They maintain their own membership in the group, both socially and productively.
7. They protect the group from stratification.
8. They make the group process a happy and satisfying experience.
9. They try to bring about genuine participation in policy formation.
10. They protect the stability and security of the school organization.
11. They engineer the process of change.
12. They use good manners and common sense while serving as discussion chairmen.
13. They are skilled in the arts of communication.
14. They are skilled listeners.[4]

Meaningful Work Strengthens Morale

For the teacher in the Christian school undoubtedly the greatest thrust for high morale comes from the sense of being a co-worker with God in the important task of nurturing young people in the Christian faith. This sense of a high calling enables many persons to accept salaries and working conditions that would be a low morale factor in another setting. Christian school employees find their morale sagging most when school conditions or attitudes of persons in the school community make them raise questions about the significance of their efforts. To be unappreciated for the work one is doing causes one to question its value and to be easy prey for temptations to be dissatisfied with other aspects of the job situation. For example, some years ago a young teacher confided that she had difficulty paying her college debts and felt unable to buy a dependable used car. However, her students were driving with their parents to Florida for extended Christmas vacations in new cars. She wondered then if Christian education was worthwhile. She also found herself tempted to have a critical and bitter spirit toward the total school effort.

In such a situation the principal will support the staff by encouragement. He will help them to open their eyes to the works of God within the school. But he will not stop there. He will truly be the school leader in raising the awareness level and commitment of board and parents to the sacrifices required of everyone to provide quality Christian education. He may even need to seek forgiveness before God for having been too lethargic in his leadership. The goal of Christ-centered education must have the backing of parents first; then board, staff, church leaders, and students will join in a hand-joined-in-hand endeavor that knows no bounds of enthusiasm.

Reviewing Morale Factors

Every principal needs periodically to review the school policies and practices to see if they are designed to make the employees happy in their work and if they are actually accomplishing what they were designed to do. Are salaries adequate? Are they fair in relation to the incomes of a cross-section of parents? Are the fringe benefits covering actual teacher needs? Are the contracts clearly written? Do teachers have academic freedom? Does the school have a code of professional ethics that all live by? Are working conditions pleasant and work loads reasonably equal? Do staff members participate in decision-making?

Nevertheless, the most important determinant of staff morale is the quality of relationships they perceive themselves to have with each other, with the principal, and with the board. As staff size grows, the principal needs to give increased attention to building these relationships.

Athletic Team Analogy

If the staff is to become a team:
1. There must be total commitment to the Christian philosophy that undergirds the school.
2. There must be confidence in the team manager (principal).

3. There must be confidence and trust in the abilities of the other members of the team.
4. There must be role definitions so that each staff member knows his own role and the role of each teammate.
5. There must be "coaching" so that everyone knows the rules of the game and frequent "time-outs" to revise strategy.
6. Suggestions from team members must be welcomed, evaluated, and used.
7. There must be a willingness to see persons with special skills put into positions in which those skills are best used for the team.
8. They must believe that the coach is not using them to build a name for himself but to promote the group individually and as a team.
9. They need the assurance that they will not be dropped from the team unless they are not playing with competence and then only if they have been instructed in how to improve.

Finally

If you can't stand the heat, get out of the kitchen!

BUT

If God has called you to this ministry, He will make strong your willing heart and mind.

TOGETHER

by Rudyard Kipling

When crew and captain understand each other to the core

It takes a gale and more than a gale to put their ship ashore;

For the one will do what the other commands although they
are chilled to the bone,

And both together can live through weather that neither
could face alone.

Notes

CHAPTER ONE

[1]Eastern Mennonite College, *EMC Bulletin,* April, 1975, p. 8.

[2]William B. Castetter, *The Personnel Function in Educational Administration* (New York: Macmillan Publishing Co., Inc., 1971), p. 16.

[3]Jay E. Greene, *School Personnel Administration* (Philadelphia: Chilton Book Company, 1971), p. 1.

[4]*Ibid.,* p. 26.

CHAPTER THREE

[1]Willard S. Elsbree and E. Edmund Reutter, Jr., *Staff Personnel in the Public Schools* (New York: Prentice-Hall, Inc., 1954), p. 59.

CHAPTER SIX

[1]Greene, *op. cit.,* p. 242.

[2]Castetter, *op. cit.,* p. 144.

CHAPTER EIGHT

[1]"Management Memo" No. 365, The Economics Press, Inc., Fairfield, New Jersey: 1976.

CHAPTER NINE

[1]William B. Castetter, *op. cit.,* p. 25.

[2]Fred B. Chernow and Carol Chernow, *School Administrator's Guide to Managing People* (West Nyack, New York: Parker Publishing Company, Inc. 1976), p. 20.

[3]Kenneth L. Pike, "Serving Our Colleagues," *His*, February 1958, p. 6.

[4]Claude E. Schindler, Jr., "Our Ministry to the School Body," *The Christian School Administrator and Teacher*, Fall, 1977, p. 23.

[5]*Ibid.*, pp. 23-24.

CHAPTER TEN

[1]Fred B. Chernow and Carol Chernow, *op. cit.*, pp. 154-155.

[2]*Ibid.*, p. 155.

CHAPTER THIRTEEN

[1]David E. Lee, "The Principal as Morale Officer—Preventing Teacher Alienation," *NASSP Spotlight*, October, 1977.

[2]Greene, *op. cit.*, pp. 17-18.

[3]Greene, *op. cit.*, p. 18.

[4]Dale Richard Wynn, "The Challenge of Working with People," *Educational Trend*, Issue Number Five Fifty Three.